I0820937

CAREY SCOTT
DIGITAL DETOX
Devotions
BIBLE WISDOM
TO UNPLUG FROM
SCREENS & CONNECT
WITH GOD
BARBOUR
PUBLISHING

YOU are the reason we do what we do here at Barbour Publishing. We promise that we will always use our God-given talents to produce content with you in mind—and that we will remain biblically faithful, no matter what.

Thank you for being the heart of our business

ISBN 979-8-89151-269-6

Cover Illustration by Rachel Mattern

Published by Barbour Publishing, Inc., 1810 Barbour Drive, Uhrichsville, Ohio 44683, www.barbourbooks.com

Our mission is to inspire the world with the life-changing message of the Bible.

Printed in China.

It's Time for a DIGITAL DETOX!

Above all else, watch over your heart; diligently guard it because from a sincere and pure heart come the good and noble things of life.

PROVERBS 4:23 VOICE

Digital distractions are everywhere, and if we're not careful, they will disconnect our hearts from our true power source—God. As believers, we should make choices that keep Him first in our lives. Let's power down our devices so we can devote time to powering up our relationship with the Lord. Instead of scrolling through social media, let's search through scripture. Let's focus on His goodness rather than focusing on our favorite streaming services. Let's have hearts consumed with delighting Him and not always digging into online hobbies. While here on planet earth, let's keep our eyes turned heavenward.

Go ahead—unplug and let God restore you. Sit with Him and be recharged. Make the Lord a priority and find true contentment. You're invited to step away from the digital world and find rest in the arms of the Creator.

WORTHLESS THINGS

Keep my eyes from gazing upon worthless things,
and give me true life according to Your plans.
PSALM 119:37 VOICE

There are few things this world has to offer that should be considered worthy. While the world may try, nothing it holds comes close to what God and heaven promise to believers. Nonetheless, many spend their time here mesmerized by the glitz and glamour. And thus their steadfast pursuit of the Lord dwindles.

The digital world, by design, tempts us daily. It has a powerful pull because it shows us the best of what life here has to offer. We obsess over what's new and what's trending. And the more we sit in front of screens, the more we long for and covet what we don't have.

Power down those distractions and power up your devotion to all things eternal.

Dear Lord, this world has nothing for me. In Jesus' name, amen.

THE TEMPTATIONS OF SCREENS

Any temptation you face will be nothing new. But God is faithful, and He will not let you be tempted beyond what you can handle. But He always provides a way of escape so that you will be able to endure and keep moving forward.

1 Corinthians 10:13 voice

It's tempting to spend our time staring at screens. There are moments when we just want to escape the rigors of the day and numb out. And rather than be present with our families and friends, or our jobs and other responsibilities, screens entice us to escapism. They offer the opportunity to step away from real life.

When you feel the pull to soothe yourself digitally, ask God to empower you to stay engaged and be available to those around you.

Dear Lord, help me overcome the temptations of screens. In Jesus' name, amen.

PUTTING JESUS FIRST

But the Lord said to her, "Martha, dear friend, you are so upset over all these details! There is really only one thing worth being concerned about. Mary has discovered it—and I won't take it away from her!"

LUKE 10:41–42 TLB

Martha was distracted by her self-made pressure to make everything perfect and everyone comfortable. But her sister didn't take the bait. She chose to sit with Jesus and soak in her time with Him. She put Jesus first, and He commended her for it.

Today, one of our greatest challenges to spending concentrated time with the Lord is the self-made pressure to check our devices. We try to sit with Him, reading the Word and praying, but we hear digital notifications. Let's put away all items that alert us to the outside world and sit at His feet every day.

Dear Lord, help me spend time with You, device-free. In Jesus' name, amen.

UNDERSTANDING THE VALUE

Blessed Lord, teach me your rules. I have recited your laws and rejoiced in them more than in riches. I will meditate upon them and give them my full respect. I will delight in them and not forget them.

PSALM 119:12–16 TLB

The psalmist understood the value of knowing God's will and putting it into action. He wanted to learn more about them, rejoice in them, and meditate upon them. He gave them the attention and respect they deserved and held them close to his heart.

When we find ourselves wanting to engage more with screens than with our Savior, it should be a huge red flag. Our desire to know God should be as strong as the psalmist's. Facebook, Instagram, and Netflix have their place, but they should never replace time with the Lord.

Dear Lord, Your Word deserves my full respect. In Jesus' name, amen.

UNINTERRUPTED TIME

I am not trying to give you more rules and regulations. I only want to give you advice that is fitting and helpful. I want to help you live lives of faithful devotion to the Lord without any distraction.

1 Corinthians 7:35 voice

Distractions are often demonic strategies to keep us from settling in with the Lord. They are designed to pull our attention away from the eternal God and focus it instead on earthly garbage. And for many of us, it works. We scroll our way through the day, letting the world entertain us with posts that add no value to our souls.

Today, commit to taking a stand and setting your priorities in order. Be a devoted follower of Jesus, and let your actions prove it.

Dear Lord, let my desired and designated time with You be uninterrupted. In Jesus' name, amen.

WHO WILL YOU SERVE?

No one can serve two masters. If you try, you will wind up loving the first master and hating the second, or vice versa. People try to serve both God and money—but you can't. You must choose one or the other.

MATTHEW 6:24 VOICE

Just as you can't serve both God and money, you can't effectively serve both God and screens. One will get your time, and the other will come in second place. One will absorb your energy, and the other will get pushed down the priority list. And whoever gets your time gets your heart.

Decide to serve God above everything else, including every digital distraction that vies for your attention. Choose your relationship with the Lord first, and watch as He blesses you for it.

Dear Lord, I choose You! In Jesus' name, amen.

THE TANGLE OF WORRY

Here is the bottom line: do not worry about your life. Don't worry about what you will eat or what you will drink. Don't worry about how you clothe your body. Living is about more than merely eating, and the body is about more than dressing up.

MATTHEW 6:25 VOICE

Social media has a way of making us worry. We see all *they* have and think we're missing out. We see *their* perfect family and realize ours is not. We read about the wonderful happenings in *their* lives, not ours. And it tangles us up.

When we let social media help define who we are or are not, it stirs up worry. So put down your phone and pick up the Bible. Let God remind you of who He created you to be.

Dear Lord, keep me untangled from digital-induced worries. In Jesus' name, amen.

LETTING GOD COMFORT

Worrying does not do any good; who here can claim to add even an hour to his life by worrying?

Matthew 6:27 voice

Have you felt apprehensive or stirred up after spending time on screens? Whether it's the trendy show on Netflix, short videos on Instagram, or posts from people we know on Facebook, we can sometimes be left feeling unsettled. We are bothered or find ourselves battling fear and stress from what we've seen. It's not healthy.

The reality is that too much time in front of screens creates uneasiness inside us that only God can calm. No good comes from worry. Consider detoxing from your devices and diving into the Word, where you will find peace and comfort every time. Let the Lord settle your anxious heart and bring perspective.

Dear Lord, I need the comfort only You can provide. In Jesus' name, amen.

SEEK GOD FIRST

Outsiders make themselves frantic over such questions; they don't realize that your heavenly Father knows exactly what you need. Seek first the kingdom of God and His righteousness, and then all these things will be given to you too.

MATTHEW 6:32–33 VOICE

Sometimes social media stresses us out because it reminds us of all we don't have. As we scroll through our favorite sites, we're bombarded by images of perfect families, epic vacations, new cars, and trendy fashion. We compare our situation to theirs and come up short every time. And we feel the lacking.

God understands the complexity of emotions social media drums up. Scripture says if we seek Him first—more than envying others—He'll meet every need. Our hearts will be changed to desire what only He can provide.

Dear Lord, help me seek You first. In Jesus' name, amen.

FOCUSING ON THE RIGHT THINGS

Finally, brothers and sisters, fill your minds with beauty and truth. Meditate on whatever is honorable, whatever is right, whatever is pure, whatever is lovely, whatever is good, whatever is virtuous and praiseworthy.

PHILIPPIANS 4:8 VOICE

God's Word is clear. He desires that we focus on the right things—things that keep our hearts decluttered by the world. Ask yourself what He considers honorable, right, and pure. Where does the Lord want you to seek what is lovely and good? What can offer you things that are virtuous and praiseworthy?

As believers, we must focus on what encourages our faith, not our love for worldly ways. Spend time in prayer and the scriptures today, asking Him to open your eyes to where they should be focused the most.

Dear Lord, help me fill my mind with what You love. In Jesus' name, amen.

ALWAYS REJOICE

Most of all, friends, always rejoice in the Lord!
I never tire of saying it: Rejoice!
PHILIPPIANS 4:4 VOICE

How can we "*always rejoice*" in the Lord when we're busy scrolling through social media or binge-watching our favorite show on streaming services? The answer? We can't. Every bit of our attention is on digital screens and not on God's goodness. Rather than praying, we're perusing. Rather than glorifying, we're googling. Instead of worshipping, we're watching. It takes our eyes and our hearts off all the wonderful ways the Lord is moving in our lives and the lives of others.

Carve time out every day to sit with God alone, without any distractions. Keep your mind focused on Him as you read the Word and pray. And always rejoice!

Dear Lord, let me see Your goodness everywhere and always rejoice! In Jesus' name, amen.

PRAY ABOUT IT

Don't be anxious about things; instead, pray. Pray about everything. He longs to hear your requests, so talk to God about your needs and be thankful for what has come.

PHILIPPIANS 4:6 VOICE

Do you ever get overwhelmed with life and look for ways to escape? Maybe you mindlessly scroll social media or lose yourself in a favorite show. The idea behind these is to literally distract you from what's heavy on your heart. You're looking for ways to forget about the challenges and struggles. You want a mental and emotional break from the weight of your circumstances. But friend, these are temporary cures that fail to comfort.

Instead, pray. Talk to God about it all. He will listen and settle your anxious heart with supernatural peace.

Dear Lord, it's only Your hand that can offer lasting peace and comfort. In Jesus' name, amen.

True contentment
comes from God
alone, not from
anything worldly.

TRUE CONTENTMENT

I know how to survive in tight situations, and I know how to enjoy having plenty. In fact, I have learned how to face any circumstances: fed or hungry, with or without. I can be content in any and every situation through the Anointed One who is my power and strength.

PHILIPPIANS 4:12–13 VOICE

True contentment comes from God alone, not from anything worldly. That doesn't stop the enemy, however, from offering counterfeit contentment through digital devices. While they may help for a bit, they'll eventually leave you feeling envious and empty by reminding you of what you don't have. You'll be left feeling undesirable by earthly standards. And the enemy wins by stirring us up even more.

Why not turn off the screen and turn to the Lord, where you're promised to find true contentment?

Dear Lord, create in me true contentment.
In Jesus' name, amen.

WHO MEETS YOUR NEEDS?

And it is he who will supply all your needs from his riches in glory because of what Christ Jesus has done for us.

PHILIPPIANS 4:19 TLB

What is it you get from the time you spend in front of screens? Do they bring peace to your spirit? Do they make you feel valued? Do they calm your worries and fears? Do they speak to the parched places in your soul? Honestly, the answer would be a resounding *no*. Any goodness they may bring wears off quickly, and you're back to square one.

Maybe it's time to detox from all things digital and sit with the one who can supply all your needs. Why not go right to God? He is your Savior and provider. He's your source and strength.

Dear Lord, You're the one who will meet my needs without fail! In Jesus' name, amen.

BOLD BEHIND SCREENS

May the words that come out of my mouth and the musings of my heart meet with Your gracious approval, O Eternal, my Rock, O Eternal, my Redeemer.

PSALM 19:14 VOICE

Sometimes we hide behind our screens and say things we'd never say face-to-face. We become bolder in arguing, more confident in saying mean things, and more courageous to speak the truth *without* love. Not only does this grieve the heart of God, but it's the opposite of His command to love others and live in peace whenever possible.

Scripture reminds us that our words matter, whether digitally or directly. And because we are believers, what we say should always bring glory to God. How are you doing with that? It may be time to take a break and refocus your heart.

Dear Lord, keep me from being wrongly bold behind screens. In Jesus' name, amen.

A POWERFUL PROMISE

Let the words from the book of the law be always on your lips. Meditate on them day and night so that you may be careful to live by all that is written in it. If you do, as you make your way through this world, you will prosper and always find success.

JOSHUA 1:8 VOICE

There's a promise attached to spending time in the Bible, chewing on scripture throughout the day, and being intentional to live in righteous ways. Doing these will bring goodness into our lives in meaningful ways. But it requires self-control.

Instead of scrolling and bingeing digitally, why not power off and open the Word? Make this powerful promise an option for you! Fill your day with learning about God's will and walking out His commands. Invest in your faith.

Dear Lord, help me choose You above all else. In Jesus' name, amen.

FAITH OR FLESH

Here's my instruction: walk in the Spirit, and let the Spirit bring order to your life. If you do, you will never give in to your selfish and sinful cravings.

GALATIANS 5:16 VOICE

Galatians 5:16 reminds us that we have a choice. Every day, we can either choose to walk in the Spirit or wander through our screens. Either our faith will rise or our flesh will lead us. And the results of this decision are in opposition to one another.

One helps to bring order to our life, while the other often leaves our spirit unsettled and stirred up. One helps us walk in righteous ways that please God, and the other promotes our selfish desires. One deepens our relationship with the Lord, while the other keeps Him distant. Which will you choose?

Dear Lord, I choose You! In Jesus' name, amen.

TRYING TO ESCAPE

God spoke to Cain: "Why this tantrum? Why the sulking? If you do well, won't you be accepted? And if you don't do well, sin is lying in wait for you, ready to pounce; it's out to get you, you've got to master it."

Genesis 4:6–7 MSG

Like Cain, when we feel God is convicting us of ungodly thoughts or behaviors, we may look for a hiding place. We may want to find distractions and diversions so we don't have to face His correction. And oftentimes, we turn to screens.

Scrolling through Instagram and Facebook can bring relief. Streaming your favorite show can help you escape momentary struggles. But these are quick fixes that won't satisfy for long. Friend, God loves you. Let Him redirect without you looking for a way out.

Dear Lord, give me a willingness to accept Your loving conviction. In Jesus' name, amen.

HINDERING OBEDIENCE

Who has impeded your progress and kept you from obeying the truth? You were off to such a good start. I know for certain the pressure isn't coming from God. He keeps calling you to the truth.

GALATIANS 5:7–8 VOICE

There are many people, pastimes, and pursuits that have the power to hinder our obedience to God. They redirect our attention from trying to live righteously by taking our eyes off Him and refocusing them on worldly offerings instead. But God continues to call you to truth.

How would your faith deepen if you powered on your faith and powered off your devices? How might you be blessed by choosing the divine over the digital? Let nothing come between you and your time with the Lord, and let nothing replace it.

Dear Lord, give me the desire to obey You over any digital distraction. In Jesus' name, amen.

INSTRUMENTS OF DESTRUCTION

But no instrument forged against you will be allowed to hurt you, and no voice raised to condemn you will successfully prosecute you. It's that simple; this is how it will be for the servants of the Eternal; I will vindicate them.

ISAIAH 54:17 VOICE

Have you ever considered that the enemy uses our phones, tablets, laptops, and televisions as instruments of destruction against us? He uses them to keep us amused and absorbed in earthly things so we don't think about or invest in eternal ones. He uses them to bring condemnation, shame, jealousy, and feelings of worthlessness. Their voices are designed to weigh us down.

This is why we must detox from them regularly, making sure their messages don't hold a greater influence in our lives. God's voice should always be loudest.

Dear Lord, give me Your wisdom and discernment. In Jesus' name, amen.

THE DAILY BATTLE

For everything the flesh desires goes against the Spirit, and everything the Spirit desires goes against the flesh. There is a constant battle raging between them that prevents you from doing the good you want to do.
GALATIANS 5:17 VOICE

Galatians 5:17 about sums it up! There is a constant battle in believers between faith and flesh, and we're fighting it every day. And one place we see it play out the most is through our digital connections.

Unless we take a stand and show great self-control, we'll get sucked into unhealthy diversions that feed our fleshly desires above all. Our faith will fail to grow. And our relationship with God will falter.

Dear Lord, open my eyes to the daily battle, and empower me to make choices that feed my faith and not my flesh. Help me want You most. In Jesus' name, amen.

WRONG PLACES

Then Jesus told them, "Truly, if you have faith and don't doubt, you can do things like this and much more. You can even say to this Mount of Olives, 'Move over into the ocean,' and it will. You can get anything—anything you ask for in prayer—if you believe."

MATTHEW 21:21–22 TLB

What a great reminder of the power of prayer. To believers, it offers an open-door communication line to God with the ability to share our struggles and ask for help. And it keeps us steadfast through the storms.

Too often, however, we take our broken hearts to social media, hoping it will make us feel better. But we're looking in the wrong places for answers to our prayers. Our hope and strength come from God alone. *His* answers are what we need.

Dear Lord, thank You for answering my prayers! In Jesus' name, amen.

THE FRUIT OF SOCIAL MEDIA

The Holy Spirit produces a different kind of fruit: unconditional love, joy, peace, patience, kindheartedness, goodness, faithfulness, gentleness, and self-control. You won't find any law opposed to fruit like this.

GALATIANS 5:22–23 VOICE

In stark contrast, social media produces envy, dissatisfaction, sadness, impatience, harshness, immorality, faithlessness, roughness, and self-indulgence. Rarely does one come away feeling better about themselves or about their circumstances. And unless we keep our scrolling time in check, it causes more harm than good.

Be sensitive to when you begin feeling these negative ways, and let it be a red flag to detox from digital exposure. Take a break altogether, or use discernment to limit your time in front of screens. Don't let anything rob you of the Holy Spirit's work in your life.

Dear Lord, I only want evidence of the Spirit's fruit in my life. In Jesus' name, amen.

SIDESHOW DISTRACTIONS

Keep your eyes straight ahead; ignore all sideshow distractions. Watch your step, and the road will stretch out smooth before you. Look neither right nor left; leave evil in the dust.

Proverbs 4:25–27 msg

Walking out a life of faith takes real grit. It requires a steadiness of trust in God, His plans, and His timing. It necessitates that we keep our eyes focused on eternal things rather than earthly ones. And the expectation is that we stay connected to the Lord in every way and every day.

Digital diversions keep us from focusing on God by sweeping us away from being present. When we sit in front of screens, we're giving our attention to sideshow distractions. Be careful and watch your step. Find the grit to keep your eyes straight ahead.

Dear Lord, help me keep my eyes straight ahead and on You. In Jesus' name, amen.

Digital diversions
keep us from
focusing on God by
sweeping us away
from being present.

FLESHLY DESIRES

Brothers and sisters, God has called you to freedom! Hear the call, and do not spoil this gift by using your liberty to engage in what your flesh desires; instead, use it to serve each other as Jesus taught through love.

GALATIANS 5:13 VOICE

What does your flesh desire? That question may be answered by what's in your social media feed or what you're watching on streaming services. And while we may know these escapes don't glorify God, we may not realize how dangerous they are to our hearts and minds.

The truth is that screens keep us in bondage to our flesh. They create an overwhelming desire for something more or different. And we are chained to obsessing over and pursuing them. Instead, find contentment in God by pursuing His plans for your life.

Dear Lord, help me live in freedom from screens! In Jesus' name, amen.

DIVINE OVER DIGITAL

Dear ones, don't be surprised when you experience your trial by fire. It is not something strange and unusual, but it is something you should rejoice in. In it you share the Anointed's sufferings, and you will be that much more joyful when His glory is revealed.

1 PETER 4:12–13 VOICE

When life punches you in the gut, what's your usual response? Where do you go for relief? Where do you turn for an escape, even if momentarily? How do you find peace and comfort in difficulties? And how do social media and streaming services fit into these worldly remedies?

Hard times should be spent in the presence of God, because He understands. Our initial surprise should be quickly followed by peace and trust in His goodness. Always choose the divine over the digital.

Dear Lord, let me always run to You. In Jesus' name, amen.

DANGEROUS TERRITORY

Most importantly, be disciplined and stay on guard. Your enemy the devil is prowling around outside like a roaring lion, just waiting and hoping for the chance to devour someone.

1 PETER 5:8 VOICE

When we allow our eyes to be overly focused on screens, it leads us into dangerous territory. It's where the enemy lies in wait to mess with our minds and hearts. We may think we're just innocently passing the time, but in reality, we're left feeling jealous toward others, distraught in our circumstances, wishing for something better, and worried for our future. And the enemy takes a bow.

Maybe it's time to detox from the digital influences in our lives and instead spend time on God-focused activities. Why put ourselves in places where the enemy can devour our peace?

Dear Lord, give me discernment to see the enemy's schemes. In Jesus' name, amen.

LET'S GET SERIOUS

We are coming to the end of all things, so be serious and keep your wits about you in order to pray more forcefully.

1 PETER 4:7 VOICE

While we don't know the day or hour of Jesus' return, we can see the stage being set. And because of that, it's time to be serious about embracing Jesus and walking closely with Him daily. Our prayers should be consistent and intentional. And if anything threatens to divert our attention, we need to turn away from it.

For most, we fall prey to distractions every day. In between meetings, as we wait in pickup lines for kids, at stoplights, or during free time, we scroll through social media. What if, instead, we prayed, opened our Bible, or engaged in a godly community?

Dear Lord, help me take my faith seriously. In Jesus' name, amen.

DIGITAL OVERLOAD

So bow down under God's strong hand; then when the time comes, God will lift you up. Since God cares for you, let Him carry all your burdens and worries.
1 PETER 5:6–7 VOICE

In those times when you feel zapped by digital overload, take your weary heart to God and tell Him about it. Unpack the ways it messed with your head and stomped on your heart. Be honest about its effects on your peace and joy. Share the hurtful messages it sent to you and the damage caused to your self-worth. Tell the Lord every burden and worry that came because of oversaturation. And then repent.

As believers, we should show great self-control when it comes to screen time. There's no doubt it often troubles our souls and crushes our spirits.

Dear Lord, keep me from overloading on the wrong things. In Jesus' name, amen.

WRONG INCLINATIONS

But when you follow your own wrong inclinations, your lives will produce these evil results: impure thoughts, eagerness for lustful pleasure, idolatry, spiritism (that is, encouraging the activity of demons), hatred and fighting, jealousy and anger, constant effort to get the best for yourself, complaints and criticisms, the feeling that everyone else is wrong except those in your own little group—and there will be wrong doctrine.

GALATIANS 5:19–20 TLB

Social media aids us in following wrong inclinations we often adopt as our own. And the verses above clearly outline what the results will be. No wonder God's greatest command is for us to love Him with all our heart, soul, mind, and strength. If that is our daily goal, we won't feel the need to invest our time in screens.

Dear Lord, keep me from being deceived by the world's digital doctrine. In Jesus' name, amen.

LOVE OVER ENVY

Most of all, love each other steadily and unselfishly, because love makes up for many faults. Show hospitality to each other without complaint.

1 PETER 4:8–9 VOICE

It's almost impossible to "love each other steadily and unselfishly" when scrolling through social media. Let's admit it's hard to see their posts promoting themselves and not feel a twinge of jealousy. We want what they have, we want to be who they are, and we want the successes they enjoy. But in those times, we often compare their very best to our very worst. We're only seeing what they want others to see. And we forget the good in our lives because we are covetous and resentful of theirs.

Be a woman who protects her heart from envy, even if that means detoxing from social media.

Dear Lord, help me love others steadily and unselfishly. In Jesus' name, amen.

SUFFERING WELL

After you have suffered for a little while, the God of grace who has called you [to His everlasting presence] through Jesus the Anointed will restore you, support you, strengthen you, and ground you.

1 PETER 5:10 VOICE

The question is, what will you do in the suffering? Because there are good and godly lessons to learn in the journey. How will you best use this time? Where will you go for hope and help? What will keep you expectant for God's goodness to prevail?

In these moments, don't sit in front of screens, waiting for suffering to pass. They offer nothing of substance for your weary heart. You may find momentary optimism, but despair soon rushes back in. Instead, pick up God's Word. There, you will find lasting encouragement and confidence.

Dear Lord, help me cling to You and suffer with purpose. In Jesus' name, amen.

WHICH PEACE?

"I am leaving you with a gift—peace of mind and heart! And the peace I give isn't fragile like the peace the world gives. So don't be troubled or afraid."

JOHN 14:27 TLB

The world's peace pales in comparison to what Jesus promises for those who love Him. It's a worthless substitute that cannot soothe an anxious heart for long. But too often the world is where we go.

What's your usual go-to? Instagram or Facebook? YouTube or Snapchat? Netflix or another streaming service? Friend, have they ever offered you peace of mind and heart that endured?

Let God's perfect peace meet you in those chaotic places and settle your spirit. Ask Him for it. Seek it. And find true and lasting contentment that never lets you down.

Dear Lord, fill me with Your peace that promises to soothe every worry and anxiety. In Jesus' name, amen.

CAREFUL AND THOUGHTFUL

If you're called upon to talk, speak as though God put the words in your mouth; if you're called upon to serve others, serve as though you had the strength of God behind you. In these ways, God may be glorified in all you do through Jesus the Anointed, to whom belongs glory and power, now and forever. Amen.

1 Peter 4:11 voice

Be careful with your words and be thoughtful in how you act, letting this mandate direct how you conduct yourself on social media. We can sometimes feel bold behind screens and respond in ways that are hurtful. We feel safe being a keyboard combatant, unaware of the depth of damage we're inflicting.

If we can't glorify God in our posts and responses, it's time to step away from digital interactions.

Dear Lord, give me discernment in my online behavior. In Jesus' name, amen.

If we're listening,
He will help us
conduct ourselves
in good and godly
ways when on
social media.

THE SPIRIT'S LEADING

If we are living now by the Holy Spirit's power, let us follow the Holy Spirit's leading in every part of our lives. Then we won't need to look for honors and popularity, which lead to jealousy and hard feelings.

GALATIANS 5:25–26 TLB

Yes, we are to follow the Holy Spirit's lead even in our online conversations. If we're listening, He will help us conduct ourselves in good and godly ways when on social media. He will stop us from saying things that are unproductive or mean-spirited. And the Spirit will keep us humble and honest as we share about ourselves.

God wants our lives—every part of them—to honor Him. We are to love others in meaningful ways and be a source of encouragement. And His Spirit will empower us to do so.

Dear Lord, I'm listening for Your leading.
In Jesus' name, amen.

WITH EVERY PART

For God has bought you with a great price. So use every part of your body to give glory back to God because he owns it.

1 CORINTHIANS 6:20 TLB

Because of Jesus' sacrifice of His body and what it did to secure your eternity in heaven, God wants you to remember the cost and honor it every day. So, how can you give glory back to Him with your body when it comes to your online presence?

You can limit the time you spend in front of screens, making sure He is number one in your heart. You can step away when you begin to feel unsettled and stressed from it. You can invest in your relationship with God first and foremost.

Dear Lord, I want to honor You with every part of myself and every part of my life. In Jesus' name, amen.

STAYING FOCUSED

My son, stay focused; listen to the wisdom I have gained; give attention to what I have learned about life so you may be able to make sensible judgments and speak with knowledge.

PROVERBS 5:1–2 VOICE

Staying focused on growing our faith isn't easy. It's not a natural response in our human flesh. We are drawn to what the world can offer us, subscribing to cultural trends and societal standards. And we align our hearts with all the wrong things.

As our Father, however, God wants us to mature our faith and deepen our relationship with Him. He wants our focus to be eternal pursuits because it helps us live in ways that glorify Him and bless us.

Put down your device, turn off your screens, and spend your time learning and living rightly.

Dear Lord, help my heart align with Your will and ways. In Jesus' name, amen.

INTEGRITY AT WORK

Work hard so God can say to you, "Well done." Be a good workman, one who does not need to be ashamed when God examines your work. Know what his Word says and means.

2 Timothy 2:15 TLB

How often do you sneak screen time when you should be working? Do you struggle to stay focused on the task at hand because you're scrolling social media or catching up on your favorite show? Be it a missionary in the field, cashier at a store, assistant to the boss, top-performing sales executive, or business owner, we should have integrity in our work. Our efforts should consistently benefit the company and glorify God, allowing us to stand blameless to both.

If you're struggling, put away all digital distractions and commit yourself wholeheartedly to what's expected.

Dear Lord, let integrity at work be a priority. In Jesus' name, amen.

SPEAKING OUT

But if you should suffer for being a Christian, don't think of it as a disgrace, as it would be if you had done wrong. Praise God that you're permitted to carry this name.

1 PETER 4:16 VOICE

Do you share online your belief in Jesus? Do you use social media as a platform to talk about your faith? Are you vocal in online interactions regarding your love and devotion to God? Good! Then chances are you've been ridiculed, criticized, and belittled for it too. Know He is pleased with your strength to speak out.

But friend, there may come a time when you need to take a break and let God heal your hurts and restore you for the digital battlefield. Don't be afraid to detox for a season.

Dear Lord, what a privilege to speak out about You online. Strengthen me. In Jesus' name, amen.

KEEPING OUR EYES ON HIM

Now stay focused on Jesus, who designed and perfected our faith. He endured the cross and ignored the shame of that death because He focused on the joy that was set before Him; and now He is seated beside God on the throne, a place of honor.

HEBREWS 12:2 VOICE

The direction is clear. As believers, we're to keep our eyes on Jesus as we walk through each day. We are to look at every situation through the lens of faith, making decisions for our good and His glory. And we are to recognize His position in heaven in relation to ours here on earth. We're to worship and follow God daily.

If screens keep you from this holy pursuit, something needs to change. Your list of priorities needs to shift and adjust.

Dear Lord, keep me focused on You.
In Jesus' name, amen.

LASHING OUT DIGITALLY

When you are angry, don't let it carry you into sin.
Don't let the sun set with anger in your heart
or give the devil room to work.
EPHESIANS 4:26–27 VOICE

Sometimes our anger plays out digitally. We can blast people on social media because we had a bad day at work. Their innocent post or response receives a nasty comment from us. We may air our dirty laundry online and vent our frustrations in inappropriate ways. We effectively slime people from our keyboard. And the devil's work is done.

When you want to lash out, stay away from your devices. Put down your phone or tablet and close your laptop. Then open the Word and sit with God, confessing, repenting, and letting Him heal those wounds.

Dear Lord, give me the discernment to know when to power off my devices. In Jesus' name, amen.

ALL THINGS FOR GOOD

We are confident that God is able to orchestrate everything to work toward something good and beautiful when we love Him and accept His invitation to live according to His plan.
ROMANS 8:28 VOICE

Because Romans 8:28 is true, we can trust Him to redeem us from our screen obsession. We can trust Him to renew our hearts and minds as we're intentionally detoxing ourselves from every digital distraction. We can be confident He will give us the ability to regulate. And we can know the Lord will reestablish our priorities as we desire to put Him first.

God is not angry with you for getting tangled up in screen time, so don't be afraid to pray for His help. Let the Lord free you from the knots so you can live in freedom again.

Dear Lord, untangle me from every digital distraction. In Jesus' name, amen.

A DIFFERENCE IN MISSION

The thief approaches with malicious intent, looking to steal, slaughter, and destroy; I came to give life with joy and abundance.
JOHN 10:10 VOICE

That's quite a difference in mission. The plan of the enemy and the plan of Jesus are poles apart. One comes to kill and destroy, and the other to give life. And while the choice of who to follow seems obvious, too often, we willingly walk into destruction caused by digital overload.

There is so much more to life than scrolling on our devices. So much more to embrace in real-time, face-to-face moments with others. Let's choose to be present rather than perusing through the lives of others online. Let's connect with God in meaningful ways. This is the life He created us to live.

Dear Lord, I choose You and the life promised with joy and abundance. In Jesus' name, amen.

MOLDED

Do not allow this world to mold you in its own image. Instead, be transformed from the inside out by renewing your mind. As a result, you will be able to discern what God wills and whatever God finds good, pleasing, and complete.

ROMANS 12:2 VOICE

One of the greatest reasons to regulate and detox from social media is anchored in Romans 12:2. As we look through our favorite platforms, we're bombarded with the world's messages of value. They tell us what's acceptable and what's out. It's their plan to mold us into their shallow image. Don't let them.

But when we step away and choose to invest in our relationship with God above all else, the Spirit molds us according to His plan. We feel valued and loved as we are.

Dear Lord, help me be molded by You and not social media. In Jesus' name, amen.

GUARDING YOURSELF ONLINE

Whatever you do, do it as service to Him,
and He will guarantee your success.
PROVERBS 16:3 VOICE

When you jump online, remember to serve Him while there. Guard yourself so you don't end up in the wrong places. Your time scrolling, working, watching, or researching should bring God glory. And if it doesn't, then consider taking a break and seeking the Lord's wisdom.

Are you engaging in inappropriate conversations? Are you shopping online when you should be working? Are you streaming movies that are questionable? Are you googling topics that are a slippery slope? When you live rightly, God sees your efforts and will bless you accordingly. We all have to be online from time to time, but be careful and guard your eyes.

Dear Lord, be with me and remind me I am serving You with my online choices. In Jesus' name, amen.

REGULATING WHAT YOU WATCH

So be careful. Guard your hearts. They can be made heavy with moral laxity, with drunkenness, with the hassles of daily life. Then the day I've been telling you about might catch you unaware and trap you.

LUKE 21:34 VOICE

In the same vein, don't let your heart be dulled by watching them either. Be careful not only in what you do yourself but also in what you allow into your home through screens. God wants our hearts and minds to be focused on Him, not on movies, shows, games, and video clips that reveal ungodly behavior. These infiltrate the deep places in us, promoting anxiety and selfishness.

Instead, live a life of faith, one pleasing to the Lord. Ask Him to help you regulate what you watch. Be sensitive to the Holy Spirit's prompting. And then be obedient to His leading.

Dear Lord, let me obey the Spirit's prompting. In Jesus' name, amen.

God wants our hearts
and minds to be
focused on Him,
not on movies, shows,
games, and video
clips that reveal
ungodly behavior.

KNOWING GOD

So hear my final words, my friends. Now that I have warned you about what's ahead, keep up your guard and don't let unprincipled people pull you away from the sure ground of the truth with their lies and misunderstandings. Instead, grow in grace and in the true knowledge of our Lord and Savior Jesus, the Anointed, to whom be glory, now and until the coming of the new age. Amen.

2 PETER 3:17–18 VOICE

Since we are believers, our greatest desire should be to know God more and grow in faith. Doing this increases our wisdom and discernment so we can follow His will and ways with confidence and steer clear of sinful behavior. But it requires time with the Lord.

When we invest more in online experiences, it keeps us stunted. We're choosing the world over the one. Be on guard and devote yourselves to growing in God daily.

Dear Lord, I want to know You more and experience Your goodness. In Jesus' name, amen.

SOCIAL MEDIA TANGLES

Since we have such a huge crowd of men of faith watching us from the grandstands, let us strip off anything that slows us down or holds us back, and especially those sins that wrap themselves so tightly around our feet and trip us up; and let us run with patience the particular race that God has set before us.

HEBREWS 12:1 TLB

Social media has a way of tripping us up. We get tangled in wanting or wishing, and it leaves us unsatisfied. We struggle to be content. And quickly, we begin to covet and crave.

Don't let social media slow you down as you pursue this life of faith! Shut it down and turn to the Lord instead, knowing all of heaven is cheering you on to the finish.

Dear Lord, untangle me from the social media snare. In Jesus' name, amen.

GOD'S PLAN FOR YOU

"For I know the plans I have for you," says the Eternal, "plans for peace, not evil, to give you a future and hope—never forget that."
JEREMIAH 29:11 VOICE

Friend, that future and hope don't include an addiction to screens. God never intended for you to be enslaved by digital distractions. Instead, He created you with a plan and purpose to further the gospel by being His hands and feet. You have a role to play here on earth, and what a privilege to be used by Him.

Are you embracing that plan? Are you deepening your faith through time with God, reading His Word, and praying regularly? If screen time seems to be your top priority, why not step away and recommit your life to His plans?

Dear Lord, help me get serious about living according to Your plans and purposes. In Jesus' name, amen.

GOD'S WORD

Oh, how I love Your law! I fix my mind on it all day long.

PSALM 119:97 VOICE

What verses in God's Word matter most to you? As you work your way through the Bible, what is He speaking to you about? What words bring comfort? What wisdom have you found? How does it comfort you by bringing encouragement? Which scriptures have jumped out, catching your attention at just the right time? Are there specific passages that you chew on throughout the day? The Bible is the Lord's love letter to you, friend. It's where He reveals Himself to those who seek.

Like the psalmist, we should love the Word, and it should be something we think about regularly. It should be hidden in our hearts and easily accessible when we need it most. Let nothing else, including screen time, rob you of this gift.

Dear Lord, I love Your Word! In Jesus' name, amen.

THE LIGHT OF THE WORD

Your word is a lamp for my steps; it lights the path before me. I have taken an oath and confirmed it: I pledge to do what You say is right and just.

PSALM 119:105–106 VOICE

If honest, we'd admit times the digital world has illuminated our path forward. We've looked to it for what's trendy in hair, fashion, home decor, and vacation spots. We've listened to snippets of political ideals and made decisions based on what we hear. We've even accepted theology after hearing a thirty-second video clip from someone we don't even know, choosing to believe their take on scripture or prophesy is accurate.

Let's remember the Word is our lamp. The God-breathed scripture inside is what lights the path we're to walk in every area of life.

Dear Lord, there's no substitute for Your Word. In Jesus' name, amen.

WHOLEHEARTEDLY

Happy are the people who walk with integrity, who live according to the teachings of the Eternal. Happy are the people who keep His decrees, who pursue Him wholeheartedly.

PSALM 119:1–2 VOICE

To follow after God wholeheartedly means to do so with passion and enthusiasm. It's an unconditional and sincere pursuit born out of purpose and passion. It's a commitment to chase the Lord with all your heart. And it brings us happiness and joy.

Remember this when the digital world tries to distract you, so you follow them instead. Be resolved to have uninterrupted time with God daily, putting aside any screens that tempt you to disengage. Whether it's a time-out or complete detox, show steadfast self-control regarding your screen time and instead pursue God wholeheartedly.

Dear Lord, let my whole heart chase after You so I can be happy and content. In Jesus' name, amen.

SURRENDERING DIGITAL DISTRACTIONS

So submit yourselves to the one true God and fight against the devil and his schemes. If you do, he will run away in failure.
JAMES 4:7 VOICE

How does the enemy use screens against you? Maybe you fall into the comparison trap on Facebook, always feeling *less than* others. Maybe you waste time on Instagram, giggling over funny videos and ignoring responsibilities. Maybe you're tempted to watch shows on Netflix that have no redeeming quality. Or maybe you tend to be a keyboard warrior and respond unkindly at times.

Scripture tells us that if we surrender these digital distractions to God and instead choose to spend time loving Him and serving others, the enemy will leave. He will lose the power he once had over us. And we will thrive in victory!

Dear Lord, I surrender every digital distraction to You. In Jesus' name, amen.

THE POWER OF THE TONGUE

But no man has ever demonstrated the ability to tame his own tongue! It is a spring of restless evil, brimming with toxic poisons. Ironically this same tongue can be both an instrument of blessing to our Lord and Father and a weapon that hurls curses upon others who are created in God's own image.

JAMES 3:8–9 VOICE

Let's remember that on the other side of critical and hurtful comments left on social media, there's a person. We may feel emboldened to speak our minds as we sit behind a screen, but our words can be brimming with toxic poisons. God calls us to love others, including during every online interaction.

If you're struggling to tame your tongue digitally, it may be time to take a break.

Dear Lord, help me discern when a digital detox is needed. In Jesus' name, amen.

EVERY PART

Oh, that every part of my life would remain in line with what You require! Then I would feel no shame when I fix my eyes upon Your commands.

Psalm 119:5–6 voice

There's no shame in self-regulating when it comes to digital doings. If your desire is to have every part of your life align with God's will, then ensuring He's your top priority is wisdom. It's showing love for the Lord in meaningful ways and letting others see your passion for living righteously.

Knowing this, are there changes you should make regarding screens? Do you need to put limits in place? Friend, what would your time spent online reveal to God? If needed, ask Him for the confidence and courage to follow His will and ways in every part of your life.

Dear Lord, help me fix my eyes on Your commands. In Jesus' name, amen.

GOD MEETS YOUR NEEDS

You crave something that you do not possess, so you murder to get it. You desire the things you cannot earn, so you sue others and fight for what you want. You do not have because you have chosen not to ask. And when you do ask, you still do not get what you want because your motives are all wrong—because you continually focus on self-indulgence.

James 4:2–3 voice

Few things awaken the feeling of lacking more than social media. Scrolling through, you're bombarded with well-placed reminders of who you aren't and what you don't have. But have you talked to God about it?

Put down the screen and pick up the Word. In its pages, you'll read truth and be reminded that He'll meet every need according to His perfect plan and timing.

Dear Lord, I know You see me. In Jesus' name, amen.

Few places bring forth untruths more than our screens, because they are fueled by the world's thoughts and ideals.

THE WORLD'S LIES

Then we will no longer be like children, forever changing our minds about what we believe because someone has told us something different or has cleverly lied to us and made the lie sound like the truth.

EPHESIANS 4:14 TLB

In this life, we will be subjected to lies every day. At times, they will cause us to be tossed here and there. And few places bring forth untruths more than our screens, because they are fueled by the world's thoughts and ideals. If we invest our time there, giving it top priority over spending time with God, we will be easily swayed by the world's lies.

Ask God for strength to know when to limit screen time and discernment to see the truth without fail.

Dear Lord, keep me steadfast in my faith and to know truth from lies. In Jesus' name, amen.

FIXING YOUR MIND

Let the proud be humiliated, for they sabotage me with a lie; still I will fix my mind on Your directives.

PSALM 119:78 VOICE

Friend, commit to focusing your mind on what God says through His Word. Listen for what the Holy Spirit impresses onto your heart. Fix your eyes on where the Lord is leading you—because if you don't, you'll fall for the world's words that will lead you astray.

Facebook, Instagram, Netflix, TikTok, and YouTube will always try to pull you away and compete for your time and attention. But as a believer, you must fasten your heart to God. Consider detoxing from those screens as you reconnect with Him, aligning your mind and heart with His will and ways. Doing so will bring blessing upon blessing.

Dear Lord, help me fix my mind on You alone! In Jesus' name, amen.

YOUR NEW NATURE

Now your attitudes and thoughts must all be constantly changing for the better. Yes, you must be a new and different person, holy and good. Clothe yourself with this new nature.

Ephesians 4:23–24 TLB

As you now belong to God through the Lord Jesus Christ, remember to wear your new nature with confidence. The Spirit within is working to shift your thoughts toward the Lord. He is changing your attitudes to coincide with your maturing faith. And you're no longer the woman you were before you accepted Jesus as your Savior.

So, set aside whatever threatens to pull you back into your old life. Don't be enamored by the flashiness of social media. Don't be impressed by what the digital world offers. Instead, stay on the trajectory of this amazing adventure of faith.

Dear Lord, help me fully embrace my new nature! In Jesus' name, amen.

BE GENTLE AND PATIENT

Be humble and gentle. Be patient with each other, making allowance for each other's faults because of your love. Try always to be led along together by the Holy Spirit and so be at peace with one another.

EPHESIANS 4:2–3 TLB

Have you felt the freedom to say what you wanted and safe from persecution when hiding behind a screen? You could vehemently disagree without others looking your way or snap in frustration without it being awkward. There is a false sense of confidence that pushes you to act in ways you wouldn't normally act. Be careful.

If the online world tempts you, listen to the Spirit's warning and step away. God says to be gentle and patient. He calls you to love and be at peace.

Dear Lord, help me choose love over the momentary desire to be critical and hurtful. In Jesus' name, amen.

HELP AND HOPE

My soul is exhausted awaiting Your rescue yet I keep hoping in Your word. My eyes are strained as I look for what You promised, saying, "When will You come to comfort me?"

PSALM 119:81–82 VOICE

The psalmist knew God was his only hope for rescue. He knew the Lord would be the one to bring much-needed comfort to his weary heart. So he cried out and waited for help.

If you're feeling overwhelmed and stressed out from digital distractions, God is listening. He knows the complexity of emotions and the details of what stirred them up. He sees your anxious heart and knows how to bring peace. And God will help you create healthy boundaries with screen time so this doesn't happen again. Why not pray to Him right now?

Dear Lord, please bring help and hope to my weary heart. In Jesus' name, amen.

THE HIDDEN WORD

I have pursued You with my whole heart; do not let me stray from Your commands. Deep within me I have hidden Your word so that I will never sin against You.

Psalm 119:10–11 voice

If the Word of God is hidden deep within your heart, the Spirit will bring timely reminders when your focus on Him is faltering. He will give you that *pause* when you're watching something that isn't healthy. He'll give you a *gut feeling* when what you're planning to say on social media isn't loving or kind. And the Spirit will offer a *warning* when your screen time and God time are unbalanced. Your job is to be sensitive to this leading and obey.

Friend, are you pursuing God with all your heart?

Dear Lord, help me spend time in the Bible and hide Your Word in my heart. In Jesus' name, amen.

FRIENDS WITH THE WORLD

You adulterous people! Do you not know that friendship with the world is enmity with God? Therefore whoever wishes to be a friend of the world makes himself an enemy of God. Or do you suppose it is to no purpose that the Scripture says, "He yearns jealously over the spirit that he has made to dwell in us"?

JAMES 4:4–5 ESV

We must be so careful not to see the world as our friend. We may have to live here for a while, but it's not our final destination. As believers, we do not make this our home.

Friend, keep this perspective with respect to screen time. Be careful you don't embrace the digital world and let it be your source of joy. The Lord wants your undivided attention and faithfulness. He's a jealous God who longs to be your heart's true desire.

Dear Lord, let me love You over anything in this world. In Jesus' name, amen.

WHAT REALLY MATTERS

My prayer for you is that you will overflow more and more with love for others, and at the same time keep on growing in spiritual knowledge and insight, for I want you always to see clearly the difference between right and wrong, and to be inwardly clean, no one being able to criticize you from now until our Lord returns.

PHILIPPIANS 1:9–10 TLB

To know what really matters, think about where you spend your time the most. What takes up most of your day? Who gets your attention? What preoccupies your mind? This may be a lengthy list to compile, but for us believers, it should be topped by living out God's will.

The problem is that we get pulled by the world's wiles. Slowly, sometimes completely unnoticed, we begin to prioritize digital distractions over our relationship with the Lord. Be careful and keep God first.

Dear Lord, You are what really matters.
In Jesus' name, amen.

A DAILY BATTLE

Come close to the one true God, and He will draw close to you. Wash your hands; you have dirtied them in sin. Cleanse your heart, because your mind is split down the middle, your love for God on one side and selfish pursuits on the other.

JAMES 4:8 VOICE

It's a daily battle for every believer. Will we choose God or ourselves? Will we focus on His goodness or feed our selfishness? Will we draw close to Him or our fleshly desires? Will we spend time in the Word, in prayer, and meditating on scripture throughout the day, or will we scroll social media?

Let's be women who can easily put down our screens without feeling like we're missing out. Let's win this daily battle by putting our love for God first.

Dear Lord, it's You first every day. In Jesus' name, amen.

HELPING OTHERS

Don't be selfish; don't live to make a good impression on others. Be humble, thinking of others as better than yourself. Don't just think about your own affairs, but be interested in others, too, and in what they are doing.

PHILIPPIANS 2:3–4 TLB

God may use you to help others recognize their digital addictions. It may be your friends or husband. Maybe it's your kids who need a reset or your nieces and nephews. Maybe it's a coworker or parent. Regardless, you may have a meaningful role to play.

We're to help others live lives that are pleasing to God, not in a bossy way but in a way that shows genuine love and concern. It's an opportunity not to nag but to gently redirect. It's loving them enough to help them see they are worshipping screens and not their Savior.

Dear Lord, use me to open their eyes.
In Jesus' name, amen.

POWERFUL BLESSINGS

You were once at odds with God, wicked in your ways and evil in your minds; but now He has reconciled you in His body—in His flesh through His death—so that He can present you to God holy, blameless, and totally free of imperfection as long as you stay planted in the faith.

Colossians 1:21–23 voice

Because you're a believer, God's power is available to you. His wisdom can be your wisdom. His peace can be your peace. And because Jesus reconciled you, His Holy Spirit has residency inside you right now, helping grow and mature your faith. And with that comes discernment.

Access these powerful blessings as you navigate the digital world. Let God help you regulate in the right ways and at the right times.

Dear Lord, I never want to be at odds with Your will for my life. In Jesus' name, amen.

GODLY BOUNDARIES

Even though powerful princes conspire against me, I fix my mind on what You require. Yes, Your testimonies are my joy; they are like the friends I seek for counsel.

PSALM 119:23–24 VOICE

There is something very reassuring about having godly boundaries. Knowing that God has given us guardrails helps us feel safe as we navigate this life of faith. Following them keeps us in His will. And when we make a misstep, we can trust He will get our attention and redirect us.

Apply this to your use of screens. When it's time to detox for a season, the Spirit will tell you. When you're watching questionable shows or wrongly obsessing over social media, you can trust Him to speak up. Ask God to regulate your digital interactions and then obey when He does.

Dear Lord, I trust Your godly boundaries.
In Jesus' name, amen.

When it's time to
detox for a season,
the Spirit will
tell you.

SOCIAL MEDIA ASSAULT

My brothers and sisters, do not assault each other with criticism. If you decide your job is to accuse and judge another believer, then you are a self-appointed critic and judge of the law; if so, then you are no longer a doer of the law and subject to its rule; you stand over it as a judge.

JAMES 4:11 VOICE

James clearly tells us to be loving and kind rather than assaulting others with criticism and judgment. This is perfectly applicable to our time on social media because it can often be a war zone.

Your job isn't to disparage on Instagram. You're not the Facebook critic. And you're not the TikTok czar. If you've accepted these positions, it's time to detox and let God restore your heart so that love freely flows from it.

Dear Lord, help my words express only love.
In Jesus' name, amen.

HOLY PURSUIT

I want to know Him inside and out. I want to experience the power of His resurrection and join in His suffering, shaped by His death, so that I may arrive safely at the resurrection from the dead.

PHILIPPIANS 3:10–11 VOICE

To know God inside and out requires intentional time and attention. It takes concentrated effort in a busy world. But friend, it should be the joy of our hearts to learn about God, better understand the life of Jesus, appreciate the work of the Holy Spirit, and experience them working together in our lives.

Make this holy pursuit what drives your choices each day, especially with respect to digital distractions. If the social media you're scrolling through and the shows you're streaming don't match up with your pursuit, it's time to turn them off.

Dear Lord, bless my holy pursuit of You.
In Jesus' name, amen.

NO SUBSTITUTE

Now that you have welcomed the Anointed One, Jesus the Lord, into your lives, continue to journey with Him and allow Him to shape your lives. Let your roots grow down deeply in Him, and let Him build you up on a firm foundation. Be strong in the faith, just as you were taught, and always spill over with thankfulness.

COLOSSIANS 2:6–7 VOICE

Social media isn't how to grow your faith. Don't let images of scripture replace opening God's Word. Don't let short videos of pastors take the place of attending church. And don't trust a random message from someone you don't know to settle your understanding of theology.

Go to God. Journey with Him throughout the day in prayer. Open the Bible so He can shape your life with His words.

Dear Lord, there's no substitute for You.
In Jesus' name, amen.

FOCUSED ON WHAT'S ABOVE

So it comes down to this: since you have been raised with the Anointed One, the Liberating King, set your mind on heaven above. The Anointed is there, seated at God's right hand. Stay focused on what's above, not on earthly things.

COLOSSIANS 3:1–2 VOICE

It takes steadfast faith to stay focused on what's above, especially because we're surrounded by *earthly things*. Every day, we're bombarded with images of what the world tells us is worthy and good. We're surrounded by cultural standards that aren't God-focused. And too often, we align our hearts with it.

This is why it's important to detox from time to time. We must step away and disconnect from earthly things so we can reconnect with God's truth. It's how we stay focused on what's above.

Dear Lord, help me set my mind on heavenly things. In Jesus' name, amen.

HE'LL LET US KNOW

So if you know the right way to live and ignore it, it is sin—plain and simple.
JAMES 4:17 VOICE

As believers who study the Bible, we should know what righteous living looks like. God's Word is clear when it tells us how to please Him with our words and actions. But still, we sit in front of screens and subscribe to what they promote, even when we know it doesn't glorify the Lord.

Let's remember that His Spirit is with us always. When on social media, He's seeing the same images. He knows what we're posting. As we watch television, He's fully aware of what's on the screen. The Spirit knows how much time we're wasting. And if we're listening, He lets us know when we're crossing over into sin.

Dear Lord, I trust You to let me know. In Jesus' name, amen.

THE PERFECT FILTER

Since you are all set apart by God, made holy and dearly loved, clothe yourselves with a holy way of life: compassion, kindness, humility, gentleness, and patience.
COLOSSIANS 3:12 VOICE

Colossians 3:12 is the perfect filter for anything we post on Facebook, Instagram, TikTok, and the like. We should ask ourselves if what we want to share is laced with compassion and kindness. Does it come across as humble rather than boastful? Are we being gentle in our responses or harsh? Do our words come off as intolerant or impatient?

Let's use social media as an opportunity to encourage others. Let's keep perspective so we don't use it with vengeance. Because we have been set apart by God, let's remember to glorify Him. And if we can't, then let's say nothing at all.

Dear Lord, let my words only encourage and build up. In Jesus' name, amen.

IN HIS NAME

Surely, no matter what you are doing (speaking, writing, or working), do it all in the name of Jesus our Master, sending thanks through Him to God our Father.
COLOSSIANS 3:17 VOICE

Let every post you make on Facebook honor God. When you share on Instagram, let it be done with thoughtfulness. Your TikTok account should reflect your love of the Lord. And whatever you decide to like or repost must also glorify Him.

Social media is a big responsibility and a place where the enemy tempts us to act badly. It can be a battlefield full of casualties, sometimes by our hand, and a dumping ground where we vent our frustrations liberally.

Instead, let our interactions there always be done in the name of Jesus.

Dear Lord, thank You for the opportunity social media gives me to point others to Your goodness. In Jesus' name, amen.

WHEN WE MAKE A MISTAKE

I have admitted my ways are wrong, and You responded; now help me learn what You require. Compel me to grasp the way of Your statutes so I will fix my mind on Your wonderful works.

PSALM 119:26–27 VOICE

When you make a mistake with what you watch or what you say in the digital world, confess it to God. Admit your wrongdoing and let Him bring restoration. He'll remove guilty feelings and bring comfort. He'll reestablish tenderness and compassion. And the Spirit will guide you into making things right with the Lord or with others.

Take time away from screens and open the Bible. In its pages, you'll find both His comfort and His commands. Take the opportunity to fix your mind on God's goodness and be refreshed by His healthy boundaries.

Dear Lord, forgive me and help me.
In Jesus' name, amen.

DETOXING FROM WORTHLESS AND WORLDLY

Be wise when you engage with those outside the faith community; make the most of every moment and every encounter. When you speak the word, speak it gracefully (as if seasoned with salt), so you will know how to respond to everyone rightly.

Colossians 4:5–6 voice

Let this be your rule of thumb when interacting online. What a wonderful opportunity to share Jesus with others who may not follow Him yet. Consider that maybe God has called you to the digital battlefield to help bring people to salvation.

Maybe what you need to detox from are worthless posts about worldly things. What if, instead, you focused every moment and every encounter on sharing the gospel? What if you posted about His goodness in your life?

Dear Lord, help me effectively use the digital world to share the gospel. In Jesus' name, amen.

WRONG CROWD

Oh, the joys of those who do not follow evil men's advice, who do not hang around with sinners, scoffing at the things of God. But they delight in doing everything God wants them to, and day and night are always meditating on his laws and thinking about ways to follow him more closely.

PSALM 1:1–2 TLB

Be a woman who's mindful to follow God's will and ways. Truth be told, it's not easy. But unless we stand strong for our faith, we'll easily fall in with the wrong people, including in digital interactions.

Be careful that online peer pressure doesn't cause you to act in the same ways as ungodly people. Don't follow accounts that promote bad behavior. These people are the wrong crowd and won't point you to Jesus.

Dear Lord, help me connect with others who love You and follow Your ways. In Jesus' name, amen.

LET IT BE GOD

"Be still, be calm, see, and understand I am the True God. I am honored among all the nations. I am honored over all the earth."
PSALM 46:10 VOICE

When facing a life storm, let God be who calms your anxious heart. Find a quiet place and listen for His quiet voice. Open His Word and let the scriptures wash over you. And pray about every fear and worry that are overwhelming you in that moment.

Sometimes we reach for earthly remedies, hoping they'll numb the pain. . .at least for a while. We mindlessly scroll through social media, trying to quiet our anxiousness. But friend, put down your phone and pray. Be still in His presence and find comfort in God's hands.

Dear Lord, help me seek You when I'm worried and fearful. I need Your presence most of all. In Jesus' name, amen.

ASK GOD

I cling to Your decrees; O Eternal One, do not let me face disgrace! I will chase after Your commandments because You will expand my understanding.

Psalm 119:31–32 voice

God outlines very clear commands in His Word, most of which we are familiar with. He helps us know His hopes and expectations for believers. But He also speaks to us individually as we seek the Lord's guidance. We can ask for wisdom and discernment when we need it.

Have you talked to God about your digital habits? Have you asked His opinion about the time you spend with screens and what you look at? Has His Spirit tried to redirect you? Today, pray for the Lord to reveal His desire for your time and how to use it best.

Dear Lord, I want to know Your will for my online time. I'm listening. In Jesus' name, amen.

Screens may
entertain us, but the
Bible trains us in
good and godly ways.

ENTERTAINING VERSUS TRAINING

All of Scripture is God-breathed; in its inspired voice, we hear useful teaching, rebuke, correction, instruction, and training for a life that is right so that God's people may be up to the task ahead and have all they need to accomplish every good work.

2 TIMOTHY 3:16–17 VOICE

God's Word is supernatural in the lives of believers. It helps us understand what a life of faith looks like. . .and what it doesn't. It teaches and trains, and corrects and convicts, so we can walk out our holy calling. In its pages, we learn that He is a jealous God who doesn't want to share us with the world.

Every time we prioritize our digital world over the divine Word, it's disobedience. Screens may entertain us, but the Bible trains us in good and godly ways.

Dear Lord, I love You. In Jesus' name, amen.

FOCUSING ON WORLDLY THINGS

But when he looked around at the high waves, he was terrified and began to sink. "Save me, Lord!" he shouted. Instantly Jesus reached out his hand and rescued him. "O man of little faith," Jesus said. "Why did you doubt me?"

MATTHEW 14:30–31 TLB

We can all relate to Peter's experience here. The times we keep our eyes on Jesus, spend time in the Word, and pray regularly, we're able to stay above the storms of life. But when we focus on the world—in his case the high waves—we begin to sink. We let earthly things disrupt our faith.

In those moments when we want to escape into screens for a break from our difficulties, remember Peter. Power them off and keep your eyes solely on God.

Dear Lord, there's nothing this world can offer. I want You. In Jesus' name, amen.

CHOKED OUT

And you know people who hear the word, but it is choked inside them because they constantly worry and prefer the wealth and pleasures of the world: they prefer drunken dinner parties to prayer, power to piety, and riches to righteousness. Those people are like the seeds sown among thorns.

MATTHEW 13:22 VOICE

Consider that too much time with social media and streaming services can often choke out the Word of God. They create all sorts of anxieties in us, like jealousy, fear, and worry. And they feed our fleshly desires for more, better, and different.

But as believers, we're to meditate on the Word and walk it out daily. And as we focus on learning and living it, we'll begin to prefer godliness over worldliness. Our faith will bloom.

Dear Lord, let Your Spirit prompt me when I'm being choked by digital distractions. In Jesus' name, amen.

LET NOTHING COME BETWEEN

Therefore, be very strong to keep and to do all that is written in the Book of the Law of Moses, turning aside from it neither to the right hand nor to the left.

JOSHUA 23:6 ESV

Maybe it's time to take a much-needed detox from the digital world. Yes, it's a strong move and may seem extreme to some, but there is a time and place for us to power off our screens so we can listen and obey what God is asking. We can't let anything come between our time with the Lord. And when social media becomes more important than praying or reading the Word, it's time to rework our priorities.

Ask the Holy Spirit to speak to you today and show you where change is needed regarding your online habits.

Dear Lord, forgive me for the times I've let the digital world take priority. In Jesus' name, amen.

HOPING IN GOD'S WORD

I despise those who waver back and forth, but I love Your teachings. You are my hiding place and my shield of protection; I hope in Your word.

PSALM 119:113–114 VOICE

To hope in the Word doesn't mean getting quick snippets of scripture off Facebook. It's not watching a thirty-second video on TikTok or Instagram from a pastor across the nation. And it's not watching a Hollywood production of a biblical story, taking liberties to fill in gaps as needed. While we might feel encouraged by these at times, they can never (and should never) take the place of opening God's Word and digging through scripture.

It's in its pages that the Lord speaks to us and offers comfort and confidence and security in our faith.

Dear Lord, there is no substitute for finding hope directly in the pages of Your Word. In Jesus' name, amen.

DON'T BE A FOOL

He who loves money shall never have enough.
The foolishness of thinking that wealth brings happiness!
The more you have, the more you spend, right up to the
limits of your income. So what is the advantage of wealth—
except perhaps to watch it as it runs through your fingers!
ECCLESIASTES 5:10–11 TLB

Ecclesiastes 5:10–11 reminds us that it's foolish to think money is the key to happiness. The truth is, the world cannot satisfy what only God is meant to satisfy. Yet so often, we fall into the pit of comparison and covetousness. Our lacking feels overwhelming.

The next time you're scrolling on social media, noticing all the goodies others have that you don't, put down your phone and thank God for His goodness. Don't be a fool.

Dear Lord, You are my source for all things! In Jesus' name, amen.

FOR THE RIGHT REASONS

People go about making their plans, but the Eternal has the final word. Even when you think you have good intentions, He knows your real motives.

PROVERBS 16:1–2 VOICE

When you choose to detox from social media, do so for the right reasons. Let it be Spirit-led. Don't do it as a show to impress others. There's no need to announce it or share the challenges it presents. You don't need to keep a video diary or a blog series to share once the time away is over. Choose to take a break so you can reconnect with God and get your priorities in order.

Use this screenless time to dig into scripture. Use it to meditate on verses. Spend time in prayer or journaling what revelations you've discovered.

Dear Lord, I'm detoxing because it's good for me and glorifying for You. In Jesus' name, amen.

ASKING FOR HIS HELP

When people make good choices, He is pleased;
He even causes their enemies to live peacefully near them.
PROVERBS 16:7 VOICE

Chances are, you pray for wisdom for your marriage or protection for your future husband. You ask for help to make the right educational or career choices. You share parenting challenges with God or ask Him to bless your desire to become a mom. You pray for financial favor and health issues. You ask for discernment regarding upcoming decisions. But do you talk to the Lord about your digital interactions?

Invite God into this part of your life. Ask Him to help establish godly borders and boundaries. Let Him help you make good choices that are pleasing and peace-promoting.

Dear Lord, I'm sorry for leaving You out of this part of my life. Help me navigate the digital world. In Jesus' name, amen.

WORLDLY BOASTFULNESS

Any place where you find jealousy and selfish ambition,
you will discover chaos and evil thriving under its rule.
Heavenly wisdom centers on purity, peace, gentleness,
deference, mercy, and other good fruits untainted by hypocrisy.

JAMES 3:16–17 VOICE

One of the most pervasive places we find jealousy and selfishness thriving is on social media. It's where people brag about who they are and what they have. There's unmatched self-promotion on TikTok, Instagram, and Facebook alike. And people use these platforms to make themselves look important, admired, popular, and grandiose.

Take a break from this breeding ground of self-glorification. Instead, fill your days with activities that usher in divine peace and purity. Spend time with people who promote good and godly ideals. Don't be tainted by worldly boastfulness.

Dear Lord, help me seek good and godly things that keep my heart aligned with Yours. In Jesus' name, amen.

TURNING HEAD AND HEART

Guide me to walk in the way You commanded because I take joy in it. Turn my head and my heart to Your decrees and not to sinful gain.

PSALM 119:35–36 VOICE

How does God turn our heads and our hearts to His will and ways? It happens as we surrender. It's a result of choosing to follow His commands over our desires. And it's not easy. Oftentimes, it requires real grit to be faithful in this way, because the heart wants what the heart wants.

Friend, if you've felt God's prompting to step away from screens and detox for a season, be brave and obey. Embrace His guidance because you will find joy in it. The Father has a great purpose in all He does, and that includes bringing you back to Him.

Dear Lord, help me obey Your promptings. In Jesus' name, amen.

PRODUCING GREAT FRUIT

I am the vine, and you are the branches. If you abide in Me and I in you, you will bear great fruit. Without Me, you will accomplish nothing.

John 15:5 voice

The only way we will produce great fruit as believers is by staying close to God. That means spending concentrated time in the Word, meditating on scripture, being prayerful, and pursuing a righteous life. That's hard to do when we're in front of screens for much of the day.

Let's detox from them and instead focus on growing great fruit through time spent with the Lord. Abide in Him so you have the sustenance necessary to mature in your faith. Screen time can be a waste of time, offering no real opportunity to produce good and godly fruit.

Dear Lord, help me focus on producing great fruit. In Jesus' name, amen.

If you're struggling
to be honest on
social media, take a
break, repent, and
let God restore you.

THE TEMPTATION TO LIE

Stop lying to each other; tell the truth, for we are parts of each other and when we lie to each other we are hurting ourselves.

Ephesians 4:25 TLB

Have you lied on social media, trying to make your life look more interesting? Have you posted pictures that make you look more attractive, or shared updates so you come off as clever or trendy? Or have you stretched the truth to make someone jealous? As believers, we have no excuse for lying, even online.

If anything tempts you to be untruthful, walk away. Don't partner with it or justify it. And if you're struggling to be honest on social media, take a break, repent, and let God restore you. He will be faithful to do so.

Dear Lord, let me walk away from anything that tempts me to lie. In Jesus' name, amen.

BACKLASH

If you find that the world despises you, remember that before it despised you, it first despised Me. If you were a product of the world order, then it would love you. But you are not a product of the world because I have taken you out of it, and it despises you for that very reason.

John 15:18–19 voice

Friend, be bold about your faith online. Speak about God, share the gospel, and unpack your testimony when appropriate. Don't back away from offering to pray for someone who's posted about a difficult circumstance. Show compassion. We can redeem social media by using it to promote God's goodness.

At the same time, be prepared for backlash. Expect it. And ask the Lord to help you navigate it and know when it's time to take a break.

Dear Lord, embolden me when the backlash comes. In Jesus' name, amen.

BEING PURPOSEFUL

It's time to stop bringing grief to God's Holy Spirit; you have been sealed with the Spirit, marked as His own for the day of rescue. Banish bitterness, rage and anger, shouting and slander, and any and all malicious thoughts—these are poison.

EPHESIANS 4:30–31 VOICE

If we cannot navigate the digital world with kindness and generosity, then it may be wise to do a complete detox from it. You may be on your best behavior in person, but it's different online. There, you're angry and mean-spirited. As believers—in every situation and circumstance—we should live in ways that please God.

It's not about being perfect. It's about being purposeful to love others as we try to live at peace with those around us.

Dear Lord, online or in person, help me be purposeful to love as You commanded. In Jesus' name, amen.

THE ROYAL LAW

Remember His call, and live by the royal law found in Scripture: love others as you love yourself. You'll be doing very well if you can get this down.

James 2:8 voice

This is a great direction to follow when we're interacting online with others. As we share thoughts and ideas—be it posting on our personal profile or commenting on the post of another—let's remember to treat others in the ways we'd like to be treated. Let's be kind and caring like we are to ourselves. And let's not try to pick fights or say something that might raise the temperature of the conversation.

If we can't live by this royal law, then we take a break. Let's remember there are real people on the other side of the conversation.

Dear Lord, help me love others through my words while online. In Jesus' name, amen.

CONDEMNATION OR CONVICTION

So there is now no condemnation awaiting those who belong to Christ Jesus.

ROMANS 8:1 TLB

There's a big difference between condemnation and conviction. The former comes directly from the enemy of your soul, and it leaves you feeling shameful and discredited. Conviction, however, is from the Holy Spirit, and it encourages you to change directions or reevaluate your decision. The first leaves you feeling rotten, and the second inspires you to live rightly.

If you're feeling the need to detox from social media, learn to discern whose voice you're hearing. God's conviction to take a step away will include an invitation to spend that time with Him. It will offer blessings from obedience. But the enemy's condemnation will be filled with guilt and blame, leaving you feeling ashamed.

Dear Lord, help me discern whose voice I'm hearing so I follow only Yours. In Jesus' name, amen.

ORIENTED TO GOD

You see, a mind focused on the flesh is declaring war against God; it defies the authority of God's law and is incapable of following His path. So it is clear that God takes no pleasure in those who live oriented to the flesh.

ROMANS 8:7–8 VOICE

One way we live oriented to the flesh is through digital distractions. They feed our desire to keep up with celebrities, musicians, athletes, influencers, and politicians. They allow us to be in a million places at once, consuming news from all over the globe. And with just a few keystrokes, we can google whatever information we're seeking.

What if, instead, we had that same fire about knowing God? What if our minds and hearts were focused on Him first?

Dear Lord, help me make changes so I am oriented to You. In Jesus' name, amen.

OPPRESSIVE REGIME

So, my brothers and sisters, you owe the flesh nothing! You do not need to live according to its ways, so abandon its oppressive regime.
ROMANS 8:12 VOICE

Just because we want something, it doesn't mean we need it. We aren't required to feed every desire of the heart. And when our flesh gets its way, it pulls us farther and farther from God's will for our lives.

If your time on social media awakens this selfishness, maybe it's time for a detox. Those platforms are full of posts that make us feel like we're missing out. They spotlight what we feel we should have. And we begin to covet. Knowing this, why participate in something that feeds the oppressive regime of the flesh?

Dear Lord, I don't want my flesh to control me. Help me choose to detox when it does. In Jesus' name, amen.

ALIGNING

Brothers and sisters, it doesn't make any sense to say you have faith and act in a way that denies that faith. Mere talk never gets you very far, and a commitment to Jesus only in words will not save you.

JAMES 2:14 VOICE

Our words and actions should align, and this includes how we navigate the digital world. If we say we're Christ followers but are mean-spirited on Facebook, how will that affect our witness? If we post scripture on Instagram but then also repost questionable material, what's that revealing? If we watch shows that cross the line with our friends or family, what does that say about our commitment to God?

Remember to align your words and actions with your faith. Your life preaches and people are listening.

Dear Lord, give me discernment so I don't act and speak against my faith in You. In Jesus' name, amen.

THE SPIRIT KNOWS

A similar thing happens when we pray. We are weak and do not know how to pray, so the Spirit steps in and articulates prayers for us with groaning too profound for words.
ROMANS 8:26 VOICE

Have you ever had trouble finding the words to pray? You try. You sit with your head bowed and your eyes closed, but you just don't know what to say in your difficult situation. So instead, you give up, grab your phone or turn on the television, and numb out.

Don't miss the opportunity to talk to the Father. Being at a loss for words should never stop you from connecting to your source for comfort and encouragement. Remember, the Holy Spirit knows your heart and will convey it all to God. So, don't reach for a screen.

Dear Lord, thank You that the Spirit knows! In Jesus' name, amen.

MAKING A CLEAN BREAK

Make a clean break with all cutting, backbiting, profane talk. Be gentle with one another, sensitive. Forgive one another as quickly and thoroughly as God in Christ forgave you.

EPHESIANS 4:31–32 MSG

When it comes to our bad behavior online, the best thing we can do to "make a clean break" from it is to commit to a detox. Sometimes it's obvious we need to step back and seek restoration from God. We need Him to soften our speech and tender our tongues so we can better follow His command to love. We need God's divine perspective to settle in our thoughts, and we need His peace to settle in our hearts. And we need to ask for forgiveness.

Detox until He tells you differently. His timing is always perfect.

Dear Lord, I'm making a clean break to be with You. In Jesus' name, amen.

PULLED AWAY

For I have every confidence that nothing—not death, life, heavenly messengers, dark spirits, the present, the future, spiritual powers, height, depth, nor any created thing—can come between us and the love of God revealed in the Anointed, Jesus our Lord.

ROMANS 8:38–39 VOICE

And that includes every digital distraction out there too. While we know for certain our time online won't affect God's love, it can distance us from His will if we let it. You were created on purpose and for a purpose. Too much time scrolling through social media or streaming your favorite shows takes time away from that purpose because it pulls you away from Him.

Limit your digital world so you can grow your faith. Prioritize your relationship with God more than anything else.

Dear Lord, help me always prioritize time with You. In Jesus' name, amen.

YOU ARE KNOWN

"I knew you before you were formed within your mother's womb; before you were born I sanctified you and appointed you as my spokesman to the world."
JEREMIAH 1:5 TLB

The Lord has always known you. He created you on purpose. You're a unique creation thought up by a loving God. So, friend, don't let anyone on social media tell you any differently. No matter the names they call you, no matter how badly they criticize, regardless of how they make fun of you, remember you are known by God. You're special and loved. And it's time you step away from that digital battlefield.

Social media has a dark side, and the enemy uses it to discourage and distract. But that doesn't change the truth of who you are because of Jesus.

Dear Lord, I know I'm loved and known by You. In Jesus' name, amen.

No matter the
names they call
you, no matter how
badly they criticize,
regardless of how
they make fun of
you, remember you
are known by God.

FAITH SHOWS ITSELF

The fact is, faith has to show itself through works performed in faith. If you don't recognize that, then you're an empty soul.

JAMES 2:20 VOICE

Your salvation has nothing to do with works. You literally cannot do anything to secure your eternity in heaven. It's by grace alone. But your faith will be proven authentic by your words and actions. Your heart will be so filled with gratitude that it'll spill out in love and compassion toward others.

This is true for how you navigate online too. Your allegiance to God should shine through in every interaction. Be kind and generous. Be tender and encouraging. And when you're tempted to be anything other than that, take a break and ask the Lord for help. You're not perfect, but you are to live with purpose.

Dear Lord, let my faith shine online. In Jesus' name, amen.

BE THOUGHTFUL

Don't live carelessly, unthinkingly. Make sure you understand what the Master wants.

EPHESIANS 5:17 MSG

This is a good rule for navigating online interactions. It's important to be thoughtful in every post and response because if not, careless words can easily slip out. There needs to be good and godly intentions behind what you say and how you say it. Because God has called us to love others, we need to remember this as we network.

In those times when you can't speak kindly or respectfully, power down your device. Know your limits and log off. Leave those frustrating platforms. It's okay to step away, especially when you're doing so proactively. He will bless you for showing discernment. Yes, God will honor your restraint as He comforts you.

Dear Lord, help me be thoughtful as I navigate online conversations. In Jesus' name, amen.

TRICKED

But now I'm afraid that as that serpent tricked Eve with his wiles, so your hearts and minds will be tricked and you will stray from the single-minded love and pure devotion to Him.

2 CORINTHIANS 11:3 VOICE

How does social media trick you? How does it lead you away from God and toward worldly offerings? We can start down a path of destruction without even realizing it. Just like he did with Eve, the enemy is always looking for ways to change your focus away from faith and onto fleshly desires.

Let's set limits. What content is out of bounds? What sites do we stay away from? How much time will we allow for screens daily? What red flags should we be watching for? And are there times we detox or walk away altogether?

Dear Lord, show me how to protect myself online. In Jesus' name, amen.

A TANGLED HEART

But the things of this life—the worries, the drive for more and more, the desire for other things—those things cluster around close and choke the life of God out of them until they cannot produce.

MARK 4:19 VOICE

There's no doubt that digital distractions play a huge role in our unhappiness, bringing with them a cluster of worries, envy, frustrations, pain, and the drive for more. Social media scrolling tangles our hearts, and rather than cry out for God, we cry ourselves to sleep. We become ineffective and shut down.

Let this be a red flag to take a break from the digital world. It's overwhelming to be inundated with so many diversions, many of which steal our peace and contentment. Open the Bible, spend time with God, and find rest.

Dear Lord, untangle my heart so I can find rest. In Jesus' name, amen.

STAND SAFE

Last of all I want to remind you that your strength must come from the Lord's mighty power within you. Put on all of God's armor so that you will be able to stand safe against all strategies and tricks of Satan.

EPHESIANS 6:10–11 TLB

Not all the digital world is troublesome. There are ministries that can reach the masses because of it. Church services can be viewed from home if you're sick or from the beach if you're on vacation. God definitely uses the internet to spread the gospel far and wide. As believers, we just need to use discernment so we can stand safe against demonic strategies.

Use your time online wisely. Ask the Lord for godly guardrails to keep you protected. And find faith-filled accountability partners, if needed.

Dear Lord, help me stand safe online. In Jesus' name, amen.

DIVINE DISCERNMENT

No wonder they are so good at it. Satan himself poses as a messenger of heavenly light, so why should we expect less from his servants—plodding over the earth, pretending to be ministers of righteousness—but in the end, they'll get what's coming to them.

2 CORINTHIANS 11:14–15 VOICE

Sometimes what we see online seems good, but it's not. Satan and his minions are crafty in their efforts to derail believers, so we need divine discernment as we enter the digital world. Watch for false teachers pushing false doctrine. Remember, just because it's on the internet doesn't mean it's true. It's a playground for the enemy whose sole purpose is to kill, steal, and destroy. Be discerning as you scroll, and step away if the Spirit warns you.

Dear Lord, let me have divine discernment so I know the truth from lies. In Jesus' name, amen.

THE CALL TO DENY

To win the contest you must deny yourselves many things that would keep you from doing your best. An athlete goes to all this trouble just to win a blue ribbon or a silver cup, but we do it for a heavenly reward that never disappears. So I run straight to the goal with purpose in every step.

1 CORINTHIANS 9:25–26 TLB

For many, the reality is that we're addicted to screens. From the moment we wake up until we close our eyes at night, our day is filled with digital distractions. And they refocus our attention away from following God's will for our lives.

Paul says we're to deny ourselves anything that keeps us from this holy calling. If the online world does that for you, it's time to make changes.

Dear Lord, help me say no to every distraction. In Jesus' name, amen.

HARNESSING FOR GOOD

Removing action from faith is like removing breath from a body. All you have left is a corpse.
JAMES 2:26 VOICE

There are terrible things about social media, but what if we choose to harness it for good? What if we detoxed from the selfish side of it and instead promoted having a servant's heart, setting up local opportunities to bless others? What if we started an online Bible study or created a support group for grief? What if we shared theologically sound sermons or our own devotionals?

Let's live our faith out loud on the platforms we love the most. We can share God's goodness with the world! He will bless our faith in action, and we might find a wonderful community of believers at the same time.

Dear Lord, help me find creative ways to harness social media for good. In Jesus' name, amen.

LISTENING ONLINE

Yet faith comes from listening to this Good News—the Good News about Christ.

Romans 10:17 TLB

There are many powerful sermon series and Christian podcasts available online. And because faith comes from listening to sound messages, take advantage of these resources! Not every digital option leads us astray. In truth, the gospel has reached so many more because of the internet. So find those trusted sites and let them bring much-needed encouragement into your heart.

If we're going to detox, let's walk away from those platforms that promote worldly messages and leave us feeling jealous or discouraged. Let's remove ourselves from places where people are up for a fight. Let's take a break from mindless scrolling or caring about what celebrities share. Instead, let's invest in good and godly options.

Dear Lord, thank You for online resources that minister and encourage. In Jesus' name, amen.

ASK FOR WISDOM

If you don't have all the wisdom needed for this journey, then all you have to do is ask God for it; and God will grant all that you need. He gives lavishly and never scolds you for asking.

JAMES 1:5 VOICE

This promise is a weighty one, and something we should take advantage of daily. No matter what we're having to navigate, God will give us wisdom so we can choose well. Why not ask Him to help you be discerning about online interactions?

Are there platforms to avoid? Are you spending too much time in front of screens? Are you heading down a dangerous path? Are digital distractions affecting your walk with Jesus? Bring your questions to the Lord and let Him infuse you with the wisdom you need for your good and His glory.

Dear Lord, I need Your wisdom! In Jesus' name, amen.

HIS BELOVED DAUGHTER

If the Spirit of God is leading you, then take comfort in knowing you are His children. You see, you have not received a spirit that returns you to slavery, so you have nothing to fear. The Spirit you have received adopts you and welcomes you into God's own family. That's why we call out to Him, "Abba! Father!" as we would address a loving daddy.

ROMANS 8:14–15 VOICE

Stand strong and confident, embracing your place in God's family. You're His beloved daughter! You have a divine purpose! So make sure your actions and words online reflect this beautiful truth.

As a family member, choose to always be a thoughtful representative in every interaction. Show compassion even when treated badly. Be kind and generous no matter what. And have the wisdom to take a break when the digital world threatens to lead you back into fear or anxiousness.

Dear Lord, I'm so happy to be Your daughter. Let my words reflect that truth. In Jesus' name, amen.

GO TO GOD INSTEAD

Happy is the person who can hold up under the trials of life. At the right time, he'll know God's sweet approval and will be crowned with life. As God has promised, the crown awaits all who love Him.

JAMES 1:12 VOICE

Some use social media to vent. They complain, hoping for sympathy or suggestions. When they lose their job, finances are in ruin, health reports are bad, or there are a myriad of other issues, they sit at the keyboard and rage. It's completely inappropriate, especially for a believer.

God invites us to cry out to Him at any time and about anything. He will strengthen us to hold up through the trials. So, stop looking for help and hope online. Instead, step away from your devices and pray.

Dear Lord, calm my heart and bring peace. In Jesus' name, amen.

ACCEPTABLE BUT NOT ADVANTAGEOUS

I can hear some of you saying, "For me, all things are permitted." But face the facts: all things are not beneficial. So you say, "For me, all things are permitted." Here's my response: I will not allow anything to control me.

1 CORINTHIANS 6:12 VOICE

While partaking in the digital world is acceptable for believers, it's not always advantageous. We can sit in front of screens all day, but is that favorable for our faith? We can make time to scroll through social media whenever we want, but is it helpful to our hearts? Is bineging Netflix constructive for our busy calendar?

This is a conversation between you and God, and one you must have. Let Him reveal His plan for your online time. And if walking away is deemed best, do so obediently.

Dear Lord, what do You think? In Jesus' name, amen.

While partaking
in the digital world
is acceptable for
believers, it's not
always advantageous.

THE FLAMING SPEARS

Don't forget to raise the shield of faith above all else,
so you will be able to extinguish flaming spears
hurled at you from the wicked one.
EPHESIANS 6:16 VOICE

When you're online, you are a sitting duck for the enemy's flaming spears. People feel emboldened to speak up and speak out against others when hidden behind a screen. And if you share your faith, post a family photo, or offer a differing opinion, it may be the spark they need to hurl insults your way.

Remember who the real enemy is. Raise the shield of faith, so their words don't puncture your heart. Let God bring perspective. And if led, sign off and take a break so the Lord can renew your strength.

Dear Lord, I will raise the shield of faith online, so the enemy is powerless against me. In Jesus' name, amen.

POINTING TO GOD

Place your trust in the Eternal; rely on Him completely; never depend upon your own ideas and inventions. Give Him the credit for everything you accomplish, and He will smooth out and straighten the road that lies ahead.

PROVERBS 3:5–6 VOICE

Do you rely on God completely? Is your trust anchored in the Lord alone? Do you clearly see that it's His goodness and faithfulness that led to your successes? Have you seen doors open and close as you follow His lead? Then share that online.

Detox from giving your own advice to others. Step back from offering your ideas and suggestions. Instead, use every digital interaction to point others to the Lord for hope and help. Share your testimony and the ways God has shown up. Point to scriptural promises.

Dear Lord, let me be a loud voice for You online. In Jesus' name, amen.

GOD ABOVE EVERYTHING ELSE

The Eternal's law is perfect, turning lives around. His words are reliable and true, instilling wisdom to open minds. The Eternal's directions are correct, giving satisfaction to the heart. God's commandments are clear, lending clarity to the eyes.

Psalm 19:7–8 voice

Let's care more about what the Lord says rather than what tries to steal our interest online. Let's open God's Word for help and hope rather than Google for answers. Let's meditate on His will above any digital offering. Psalm 19:7–8 reminds us of some powerful truths about His faithfulness and wisdom, available to all believers.

Friend, don't miss the mark. It should always be God above everything else. His ways are full of His goodness and blessings, and we will find peace there.

Dear Lord, let my Savior's words always be more important than anything on screens. In Jesus' name, amen.

EXPERIENCE HEALING

If you depend on Him, your body and mind will be free from the strain of a sinful life, will experience healing and health, and will be strengthened at their core.

PROVERBS 3:8 VOICE

As you walk out the discipline of a digital detox, press into the Lord. Draw close to Him through time in the Word. Be prayerful, confessing the strains that screens brought into your life. Be honest about every struggle you had with the sinful desires the digital world birthed in you. Pour out your heart, asking Him for comfort and restoration. Ask for godly guardrails to keep you safe.

Then watch as the Lord brings healing to your soul. He will settle your anxious heart and strengthen you at the core.

Dear Lord, be with me during this time and restore me in all Your good and godly ways. In Jesus' name, amen.

CARRIED AWAY

When a person is carried away with desire, lured by lust, and when desire becomes the focus and takes control, it gives birth to sin. When sin becomes fully grown, it produces death.

James 1:14–15 VOICE

Social media excels at carrying people away with desire. Amen? It awakens in us a longing for what we don't have. It gives us a hankering for what's just out of reach, prodding us to work harder so we can achieve it. It creates a thirst to be better and different as if who God made us to be isn't good enough. It produces a longing for all the wrong things. And when we give into those desires, and they take control, it leads us into sinful thoughts and behaviors.

Dear Lord, empower me to step away from things that are not of You. In Jesus' name, amen.

LOVING CORRECTION

My son, do not ignore the Eternal's instruction or lose heart when He steps in to correct you; because the Eternal proves His love by caring enough to discipline you, just as a father does his child, his pride and joy.

PROVERBS 3:11–12 VOICE

God corrects those He loves. And as a believer, you can expect the Lord to discipline you as needed, even in your online habits.

Are you pushing the borders with what you watch on Netflix? Are you overly interested in seeing what others are doing on Facebook? Are you wasting too much time on TikTok or Instagram, enamored by funny videos? Are your online searches heading in the wrong direction? Heed God's loving correction, confess, repent, and step away. And thank Him for caring enough to call you out.

Dear Lord, You're an amazing Father.
In Jesus' name, amen.

WHEN YOU MESS UP

In addition to all that has been said, Your servant will find, hidden in Your commandments, both a strong warning and a great reward for keeping them. Who could possibly know all that he has done wrong? Forgive my hidden and unknown faults.

PSALM 19:11–12 VOICE

In those moments where you mess up online, confess all wrongdoing to God. Don't let any time pass, because the enemy wants to bring shame and condemnation as you stay silent about those hidden searches. The Lord already knows, but He wants to hear from you.

It may also be time for a digital detox so you can spend time with God and be restored. He will get to the heart of the matter and help you understand what derailed you.

Dear Lord, I'm sorry for messing up. Please draw close and restore me. In Jesus' name, amen.

GUARDING YOUR GOOD SENSE

My son, never lose sight of God's wisdom and knowledge: make decisions out of true wisdom, guard your good sense, and they will be life to your soul and fine jewelry around your neck. Then each one of your steps will land securely on your life's journey, and you will not trip or fall.

PROVERBS 3:21–23 VOICE

When we trust God for wisdom as we go online, He will help guard our good sense. The Spirit will keep us from tripping.

The reality is there's endless freedom on the internet. We can search for anything of interest from the comfort of our homes—wholesome or inappropriate—with no one watching where we go. This is why we need to invite God into every digital interaction and ask for true wisdom.

Dear Lord, be with me as I navigate the digital world. In Jesus' name, amen.

BENT TOWARD PRIDE

As I am Your servant, protect me from my bent toward pride, and keep sin from ruling my life. If You do this, I will be without blame, innocent of the great breach.

PSALM 19:13 VOICE

Have you ever bragged about something on social media? Be it a job promotion, a new car, a kid's college acceptance letter, or a new coat of paint, there's a fine line between sharing news and boasting. These platforms are often used to promote yourself to the world, and at times, pride is the motivation.

Listen to the Holy Spirit's leading before you post anything. Ask Him to give you keen discernment if this is something to share or not. And if so, let your words and images be thoughtful and modest.

Dear Lord, keep me humble in what I choose to share. In Jesus' name, amen.

GOOD AND PERFECT

My dearly loved brothers and sisters, don't be misled. Every good gift bestowed, every perfect gift received comes to us from above, courtesy of the Father of lights. He is consistent. He won't change His mind or play tricks in the shadows.

JAMES 1:16–17 VOICE

Have you considered that a digital detox could be a good and perfect gift from above? It may be exactly what you need to calm anxiety. If social media has captured your days and streaming services your evenings, God knows your need for redirection and restoration. If scrolling has brought feelings of jealousy or unworthiness, He'll cleanse your heart. The Lord will bless you by removing the pollutants that unsettle your spirit.

It's a good and perfect gift to step away and detox.

Dear Lord, thank You for loving me enough to call me away with You. In Jesus' name, amen.

Let our attention
be on pleasing
God, not sitting in
front of screens.

MINIMALIST MINDSET

You see we came into this world with nothing, and nothing is going with us on the way out! So as long as we are clothed and fed, we should be happy.

1 Timothy 6:7–8 VOICE

This minimalist mindset is a great way for believers to think. Rather than collecting treasures here, our focus should be on storing eternal things, like loving others, serving them, and sharing God's goodness in meaningful ways. As believers, we should seek the Lord through prayer and time in His Word. Let our attention be on pleasing God, not sitting in front of screens.

Step out of the chaos they bring, avoid the trap of comparison, and let go of the desire to collect worldly stuff. You can't take any of it with you.

Dear Lord, remind me that I can't take any worldly things with me! In Jesus' name, amen.

HUMAN INTERACTIONS FIRST

Do not withhold what is good from those who deserve it; if it is within your power to give it, do it. Do not send your neighbor away, saying, "Get back with me tomorrow. I can give it to you then," when what he needs is already in your hand.

PROVERBS 3:27–28 VOICE

If you're able to help someone who needs it, generously make the time. Not only does that act of love bless them, it also delights the heart of God. It may require you to step away from the online world to serve them. You may have to give up movie night or shopping for online deals. But Proverbs 3:27–28 reminds us to be helpful even if it's inconvenient.

God would never want digital distractions to keep us from human interactions.

Dear Lord, help me love and serve others first. In Jesus' name, amen.

CHASING RICHES

But those who chase riches are constantly falling into temptation and snares. They are regularly caught by their own stupid and harmful desires, dragged down and pulled under into ruin and destruction.

1 TIMOTHY 6:9 VOICE

Social media has a sneaky way of making us chase riches. As people are posting and boasting online about their stuff, it awakens our wanting. We covet, becoming discontented. We complain about lack of money, grumble over what we don't have, and adopt an attitude of entitlement. We fall right into the snares of the enemy.

Friend, shut down the online sites that create this mindset. This isn't how believers should feel. God knows what we need and will provide for us at the right time and in the right ways.

Dear Lord, forgive me for my wrong attitude. I trust You to provide as You see fit. In Jesus' name, amen.

GRABBING YOUR ATTENTION

But Lot kept procrastinating, so the two heavenly messengers grabbed him, his wife, and his two daughters by the hand. They took them outside the city, a safe distance away, because the Eternal decided to show mercy to Lot and his family.

GENESIS 19:16 VOICE

Like Lot and his family, we can also find ourselves procrastinating because we're sidetracked by worldly things. And one of the biggest offenders is digital distractions. It can be an unhealthy focus that requires God's intervention to break free from. We need the Lord to grab our attention.

Maybe you've felt the Holy Spirit's prompting to take a break because screens have been a source of frustration lately. Don't ignore it. God may be calling you to leave them for a time as an act of mercy.

Dear Lord, I hear You. In Jesus' name, amen.

GETTING AWAY

Then Jesus suggested, "Let's get away from the crowds for a while and rest." For so many people were coming and going that they scarcely had time to eat.

Mark 6:31 TLB

If Jesus saw the need for a detox, then certainly, we can see the need for one too. Doing so enables us to get away from online crowds and the rat race that ensues. We get to remove ourselves from triggers that disturb our peace. Stepping away allows us to regain a good and godly perspective. And when we are purposeful to take a break, our spirit finds rest in God's presence.

Is it time for a detox? Are you ready for a change of pace? Are you tired of being digitally bombarded? Follow Jesus' example and get away from the crowds for a time.

Dear Lord, I'm following Your example.
In Jesus' name, amen.

PUT INTO ACTION

Put the word into action. If you think hearing is what matters most, you are going to find you have been deceived.

JAMES 1:22 VOICE

If you say you're a believer, let your actions back it up. Be bold in your faith! We're not to just hear the Word of God; we're to put it into action every day. Be very careful, friend. Nothing can ruin your testimony more than spewing rude or hateful words toward others online. You can't quote a scripture on Monday, post a sermon on Tuesday, and then rake someone over the coals on Wednesday.

Maybe it's time for a break so you can regroup and reconnect with the Lord. Maybe step away altogether from certain platforms that trigger you. Follow God's command as you navigate the online minefield.

Dear Lord, help me put my faith into action online. In Jesus' name, amen.

HOLY PURSUIT

For the love of money—and what it can buy—is the root of all sorts of evil. Some already have wandered away from the true faith because they craved what it had to offer; but when reaching for the prize, they found their hands and hearts pierced with many sorrows.

1 Timothy 6:10 voice

Sometimes people post about new cars or fancy vacations. They share pictures of home renovations or backyard expansions. And online algorithms know what products to push our way. It awakens our desire for more money to buy what we don't need.

We should be craving more of God instead, longing for uninterrupted time with Him. Our greatest desire should be growing closer to the Lord and living righteously. Shut down whatever usurps this holy pursuit.

Dear Lord, forgive me for wanting anything more than You. In Jesus' name, amen.

YOUR SOURCE

So don't be afraid. I am here, with you; don't be dismayed, for I am your God. I will strengthen you, help you. I am here with My right hand to make right and to hold you up.

Isaiah 41:10 voice

Where do you need strength and comfort today? What feels overwhelming? Where are you craving guidance and wisdom? If you're looking to TikTok, Instagram, or Facebook for encouragement, you won't find it. They cannot meet those deeper needs.

Instead, go right to your source for all things. Power down your devices and open the Word of God. Pray to Him in earnest, sharing your heart and asking for help. Sit and wait with expectation. And quiet yourself from every worldly voice so you can hear His.

Dear Lord, You are my source for all things. Nothing in this world even comes close. In Jesus' name, amen.

DIVIDING BELIEVERS

If anyone teaches a different doctrine and does not agree with the sound words of our Lord Jesus Christ and the teaching that accords with godliness, he is puffed up with conceit and understands nothing. He has an unhealthy craving for controversy and for quarrels about words, which produce envy, dissension, slander, evil suspicions.

1 TIMOTHY 6:3–4 ESV

Social media can be a useful tool for sharing the gospel. We can access sermons from pastors all over the world at any time. It's allowed us to connect with the global church and encourage one another. But be sure you check any message against God's Word. False teachers and false doctrine are running rampant these days, and they divide believers.

If their words and actions don't align with the Bible, turn them off and walk away.

Dear Lord, give me discernment to know when to walk away from divisive people. In Jesus' name, amen.

GRAVITATIONAL PULL

However, it is possible to open your eyes and take in the beautiful, perfect truth found in God's law of liberty and live by it. If you pursue that path and actually do what God has commanded, then you will avoid the many distractions that lead to an amnesia of all true things and you will be blessed.

James 1:25 voice

When we're enraptured by all the happenings on social media, it's easy to lose track of time. We feel the gravitational pull of Facebook, TikTok, and Instagram that keeps us scrolling. But from whom or what are we stealing time to do so? What responsibilities are we shirking? To whom are we not giving our time and attention?

It may be time for a break.

Dear Lord, help me follow Your plan so I don't get caught up in distractions. In Jesus' name, amen.

THE PRODDING

The prodding of my heart leads me to chase after You.
I am seeking You, Eternal One—don't retreat from me.
PSALM 27:8 VOICE

Have you been feeling the prodding of the Holy Spirit to put down your devices and spend more time with God? When you jump into the digital world, is it less satisfying? Are you struggling to find shows to watch in the evening? Do you lack interest in checking the updates of those you follow? Maybe the Lord is trying to get your attention.

Why not take this opportunity to sit with Him, committing to spend extra time in the Word? Why not talk to God more? Chase after Him because He has something wonderful for you, and you won't want to miss it.

Dear Lord, thank You for wanting to spend more time with me! In Jesus' name, amen.

ETERNITY

I am pleading with the Eternal for this one thing,
my soul's desire: to live with Him all of my days—
in the shadow of His temple, to behold His beauty and
ponder His ways in the company of His people.

Psalm 27:4 voice

We can't even begin to understand the awesomeness of our eternal home in heaven. Our minds are unable to comprehend what it will be like. But it's real, and it's wonderful, and we will experience it. And thankfully, we'll leave every single worry of this world behind.

So, let's not get too caught up in our lives here or the worries of today. Let's not care so much about social media or our favorite shows. Put those aside and sit in wonder of what's coming.

Dear Lord, the digital world holds nothing for me when compared to eternity. In Jesus' name, amen.

DISCONTENTED

Keep your lives free from the love of money, and be content with what you have because He has said, "I will never leave you; I will always be by your side."

HEBREWS 13:5 VOICE

It's hard not to covet when we see people online bragging about their new toys. When they post vacation pictures, but we're stuck in the daily grind, we long for a getaway. And every time we jump online, we are bombarded with ads for new products that create a *must-have* mentality. It makes us discontented with what we already have. It just never seems to be…enough.

Money itself isn't the problem; it's when we love it. Friend, if time on screens is stealing your contentment, power them down. Put them away. And talk to God, thanking Him for the ways He's blessed you.

Dear Lord, I am content in You. In Jesus' name, amen.

THE WRONG PATH

I have wandered down the wrong path like a lost sheep; come find me, Your servant, because I do not forget Your commands.

Psalm 119:176 VOICE

You can cry out for God's help at any time. That includes when you've been stuck scrolling online and saw something upsetting. Maybe it's a group picture that didn't include you or a celebration you weren't invited to. Maybe someone's child had remarkable success while yours is struggling to find footing. Maybe you wandered into spaces with immoral content. Regardless, when you've wandered down the wrong path online, stop, shut it down, and pray.

Consider taking a break and letting God restore you. Get back into the Word and find comfort. And create boundaries to keep you safe.

Dear Lord, when I wander down the wrong path online, thank You for promising to find and restore me. In Jesus' name, amen.

When you've
wandered down
the wrong path
online, stop, shut it
down, and pray.

CONTROLLING YOUR MOUTH

If you put yourself on a pedestal, thinking you have become a role model in all things religious, but you can't control your mouth, then think again. Your mouth exposes your heart, and your religion is useless.

JAMES 1:26 VOICE

Be careful that you don't ruin your witness by letting your mouth run loose online. When you share scripture or post sermons one day but then tear someone to shreds for having a different opinion the next, it shocks people. It confuses them about who you truly are. And that tongue-lashing exposes your heart.

Let God work to tender your heart and heal it. Let Him reveal places in you that need His attention. And until then, step away from any online interactions that stir you up.

Dear Lord, forgive my hurtful words. My heart is heavy, and I need Your healing. In Jesus' name, amen.

EAGERLY WAITING?

But we are citizens of heaven, exiles on earth waiting eagerly for a Liberator, our Lord Jesus the Anointed, to come and transform these humble, earthly bodies into the form of His glorious body by the same power that brings all things under His control.

PHILIPPIANS 3:20–21 VOICE

Are you waiting eagerly to see Jesus face-to-face? Are you spending this time wisely? Do your actions reveal that expectation?

Let's not be wasteful while here. Our job is to share the gospel and bring glory to God's name. Our words and actions should point to the Lord in heaven. If we're spending all day mindlessly staring at screens, we're not waiting well. Let's power down our devices and make our time count. Let's be bold for Christ and share Him with others.

Dear Lord, let my life bring You glory in every way. In Jesus' name, amen.

WITH A KIND HEART

Brothers and sisters, don't waste your breath complaining about one another. If you judge others, you will be judged yourself. Be very careful! You will face the one true Judge who is right outside the door.

JAMES 5:9 VOICE

We're to love, plain and simple. It's not an easy command to walk out, but it's expected of believers. Even on social media, God expects us to show kindness as we interact with others. That means we don't sit in judgment and criticize one another. We don't gossip or respond harshly. Let's remember that God sees everything we type, hears everything we say, and knows everything we're thinking.

If you're struggling to navigate social media with a healthy respect and kind heart, it's time to detox. Ask Him for help.

Dear Lord, help me be kind online or step away for a season. In Jesus' name, amen.

SET FREE

Give attention to my misery and rescue me because I have not forgotten Your teaching. Fight for me, and set me free; give me life in keeping with Your promise.

PSALM 119:153–154 VOICE

The psalmist obviously understood the magnificent power of God, asking Him to rescue him, fight for him, and set him free. He knew the Lord was his only hope for living a righteous and pleasing life. Friend, this divine power is still true and available to us today.

If you're feeling stuck in the rat race of digital distractions, pray for God's interaction. Maybe you can't stop measuring your value by views, likes, or reposts. Maybe you're battling jealousy at epic levels. Today, ask God to rescue you, fight for you, and set you free so you can get on with a purposeful life.

Dear Lord, free me from this digital rat race! In Jesus' name, amen.

OVERSHARING

So own up to your sins to one another and pray for one another. In the end, you may be healed. Your prayers are powerful when they are rooted in a righteous life.

James 5:16 VOICE

It's important to be transparent with one another, letting others know you're in need of prayer for a shortcoming. When you do something wrong, admit it. When you speak out of turn or share a bit of gossip, admit it. When your behavior is cruel, unhealthy, or immoral, admit it. But not on social media.

There's often a lack of discernment when it comes to what we say online. We tend to overshare, and it needs to stop. Instead, find a trustworthy friend for accountability. Be wise with what you share digitally, or step away.

Dear Lord, help me discern between online and in-person sharing. In Jesus' name, amen.

CONFESSING JESUS

Fight on for God. Hold tightly to the eternal life that God has given you and that you have confessed with such a ringing confession before many witnesses.

1 TIMOTHY 6:12 TLB

It's not always popular to be a professed Christian online. Many times, it opens you up to intense criticism and ridicule, and the Bible says this kind of persecution is only going to get worse as we approach the return of Jesus. Don't be afraid to confess the Lord as your Savior digitally or in person. Be brave and bold.

You don't have to beat people over the head with your faith, but you can (and should) live unashamed. If you're tempted to water down your beliefs online, then maybe it's time to take a break and let God restore your resolve.

Dear Lord, I am not ashamed of the gospel.
In Jesus' name, amen.

THE STING OF SOCIAL MEDIA

Trouble and distress have overtaken me,
but Your commandments bring me great joy.
PSALM 119:143 VOICE

When you feel the sting of social media—like being attacked in comments, seeing upsetting news, or feeling jealousy creeping in—turn to God. Few things can create distress in our hearts more than scrolling through updates and posts. But the Lord's presence ushers in peace and brings joy when we need it most.

Instead of catching up on the lives of your online community and feeling angst, why not sit in the Word? Let scripture remind you of your immeasurable worth and the goodness of God. Find encouragement in the stories of Bible characters who were flawed and loved. There is no better way to settle your spirit.

Dear Lord, when social media causes distress, remind me that Your Word soothes and encourages. In Jesus' name, amen.

TO PURSUE OR NOT

Brothers and sisters, if someone you know loses his way and rebels against God, pursue him in love and bring him back to the truth.

JAMES 5:19 VOICE

If you speak the truth online, James says to do so with love. It's not always appropriate, but if you feel God is leading you to connect with someone who's lost their way or is in active rebellion against the Lord, do so with His guidance.

Is your response for all to see, or is it a private message? What's the best timing and approach? Are you to pursue their restoration through prayer, asking for a heart change? Or do you need a break from the digital world because God's not calling you to confront them? Seek His path forward before you make a move.

Dear Lord, reveal Your will for my actions. In Jesus' name, amen.

IN PERSON INSTEAD

Tell them to go after God, who piles on all the riches we could ever manage—to do good, to be rich in helping others, to be extravagantly generous. If they do that, they'll build a treasury that will last, gaining life that is truly life.

1 TIMOTHY 6:17–19 MSG

We can't effectively walk out 1 Timothy 6:17–19 if we're stuck in front of screens all day long. It's difficult to lead with a servant's heart if our greatest desire is scrolling social media and sitting in front of streaming services.

So, detox from every digital distraction and engage with in-person community instead. Find ways to bless others. Be ready to help when a need arises. Show generosity with your time and treasure. Be His hands and feet.

Dear Lord, let me see the value of in-person community over anything digital. In Jesus' name, amen.

A GUIDING LIGHT

Guide my steps in the ways of Your word,
and do not let any sin control me.
PSALM 119:133 VOICE

Let this verse be a guiding light as you navigate the landscape of the digital world. Looking at screens through the lens of God's will allows your time with them to be pleasing and acceptable.

Consider how you can find the right balance between online scrolling and being in the Word. How do you know when what you're watching is inappropriate as a believer? What keeps you from adopting wrong thinking promoted by posts and videos? Are there platforms to take a break from or delete altogether because they rob you of peace and joy? What red flags do you need to watch for? Let the Lord be your guiding light.

Dear Lord, show me how to be online responsibly.
In Jesus' name, amen.

Be careful you don't
adopt the views
and theologies of
quick videos posted
by people you don't
know and trust.

SPOILING WITH WRONG ANSWERS

Don't let others spoil your faith and joy with their philosophies, their wrong and shallow answers built on men's thoughts and ideas, instead of on what Christ has said.

Colossians 2:8 TLB

Colossians 2:8 is a great reminder that there's no substitute for opening the Bible and reading His words yourself. Be careful you don't adopt the views and theologies of quick videos posted by people you don't know and trust. Don't get your scripture from attractive graphics and assume it's cited correctly. And just because it's online doesn't mean it's accurate. Believing these digital offerings may spoil your faith with wrong answers that are biblically incorrect.

The only way you can know for certain what God has to say is by spending time in His Word.

Dear Lord, there is no substitute for reading Your Word daily. In Jesus' name, amen.

TIME TO WALK AWAY

Walk away from all the godless, empty voices out there, and turn aside from objections and arguments that arise from false knowledge. (By professing such knowledge, some are missing the mark when it comes to true faith.) May God's grace be with you.

1 TIMOTHY 6:20–21 VOICE

There are a lot of godless, empty voices found on social media. Facebook, Instagram, TikTok, and the like feature many who share fake news and untruths. They spout off about faith, missing the mark of who God is and what He has said in the Word. And too often, we hear it and blindly believe it.

Maybe it's time to walk away from it, be it for a season or a lifetime. Pray and listen for His leading.

Dear Lord, show me Your desire for how I'm to engage with social media. In Jesus' name, amen.

THE ONLINE SMEAR

The proud smear me with their lies; I will keep Your instructions wholeheartedly. Their hearts are dull and callous; I am delighted to study Your teaching.
Psalm 119:69–70 VOICE

Like the psalmist who faced a smear job by hateful people, the same can happen to us with online interactions. There are those who use social media as a place to vent their frustrations and speak without compassion. They may be on their best behavior face-to-face, but they become keyboard warriors when the opportunity arises.

Rather than engage and defend, shut down your device. Vow to take a much-needed break for a time, and open God's Word. He will meet you there and provide comfort and perspective. His words will settle your spirit. The Lord will restore you.

Dear Lord, when I feel smeared, help me remember that Your words heal. In Jesus' name, amen.

PERFECT PEACE

You will keep the peace, a perfect peace, for all who trust in You, for those who dedicate their hearts and minds to You.

Isaiah 26:3 voice

We all dedicate our hearts and minds to something. And scripture says when that dedication is focused on God, we'll experience perfect peace. As we trust Him, comfort will follow.

Friend, where is your dedication today? Who or what gets the most of your time and attention? If your day is filled with digital distractions, chances are your spirit is unsettled. The amount of information that comes our way is unhealthy and creates stress. It just is too much and overwhelms us with anxiety. The remedy is to power off your devices and set your heart and mind on good and godly things instead.

Dear Lord, my heart and mind are dedicated to You alone. In Jesus' name, amen.

PURSUING GOD

"Seek the Lord; yes, seek his strength and seek his face untiringly."
1 CHRONICLES 16:11 TLB

One of the best reasons to detox from the digital world is so you can pursue the Lord wholeheartedly. You may not be aware of how many hours a day you spend in front of screens, but it's more than you realize. Think of the times you're scrolling on your phone or tablet. The amount of time you spend on your computer, working, answering emails, looking at news, or paying bills. And then there's television. Do you spend most evenings watching your favorite shows?

God wants you to pursue Him above all else. He wants you to seek His strength, His wisdom, His peace, and His comfort. The Lord wants you to *want* to be in His presence.

Dear Lord, I will set aside my screens and pursue You instead. In Jesus' name, amen.

GODLY GUARDRAILS

Help me to learn good judgment and knowledge
because I believe Your commandments.
PSALM 119:66 VOICE

Don't be embarrassed or feel it's too petty. Go ahead and ask God to empower you for sound judgment regarding your online presence. Let Him show you how to interact, how much time to spend there, and where the godly guardrails lay. Let the Spirit bring conviction if you're heading into dangerous territory. And let the Lord fill you with the knowledge on how to keep the digital world in a healthy perspective.

If you wholeheartedly seek God's will in your life, you will find it. He will show you the path forward. From career moves to financial issues to relationship challenges to screen time, ask Him to show you godly guardrails.

Dear Lord, teach me to live within Your good and godly boundaries. In Jesus' name, amen.

DON'T FALL IN LOVE

Don't fall in love with this corrupt world or worship the things it can offer. Those who love its corrupt ways don't have the Father's love living within them.

1 JOHN 2:15 VOICE

The online world's offerings may look enticing, but they're fleeting. It's fun to scroll through social media to see what others are up to. We love to see new product promotions and life hacks. It's entertaining to watch video clips of cute animals, people being silly, or the latest dance craze. But the fun feelings fade quickly, and we're left unfulfilled.

See the digital world for what it is. There's no eternal goodness found there, so don't fall in love with what it offers. And never let it take the place of your daily pursuit of God and the deepening of your faith.

Dear Lord, I love You most. In Jesus' name, amen.

THE DECEPTIVE PATH

Indeed, I love Your commands more than gold, even more than the highest quality gold. It's true that I regard all Your guidance to be correct and good; I despise every deceptive path.

PSALM 119:127–128 VOICE

As believers, we should have a strong distaste for any path leading us away from God. When something threatens our allegiance and commitment to Him, once we see what's really going on, we should return to the Lord with a repentant heart.

Have digital distractions been a deceptive path for you? Have they taken time away from Him? Have they replaced Bible reading or prayer time? Are you more interested in scrolling than sitting with the Lord? If so, repent, return, and reengage with God. Choose to love Him more than anything else.

Dear Lord, show me every deceptive path so I can stay connected to You. In Jesus' name, amen.

CHARTING OUT A PATH

I carefully charted out my paths to align my steps with Your decrees.

PSALM 119:59 VOICE

If we're careful to follow God's guidance, it will help us keep digital distractions to a minimum. He will show us how to regulate, revealing where to curb time, what platforms to disengage from, and when to unplug entirely. And He will give us the strength to make those tough choices.

Between social media and streaming services, it's easy to get swept up in them. They can be fun and entertaining! But too often, we put them above our time with God, and that's where we get into trouble. Chart out a path for moderation, and then ask Him to make any changes necessary.

Dear Lord, I want to honor You with my choices, and I trust You will rework my plans as needed. In Jesus' name, amen.

YOU HAVE EVERYTHING

Because the Lord is my Shepherd, I have everything I need! He lets me rest in the meadow grass and leads me beside the quiet streams. He gives me new strength. He helps me do what honors him the most.

Psalm 23:1–3 TLB

If you already have everything you need because of the Lord, a stream of positive responses to your Facebook post isn't needed. A certain number of views on Instagram won't make you feel loved. In Jesus, you have everything you need.

When social media becomes how you measure your goodness, it's time to take a break. Be kind to yourself and honor God by detoxing from those platforms, and let Him restore peace and give you new strength.

Dear Lord, forgive me for letting social media determine my worth. With You, I have everything I need to feel loved. In Jesus' name, amen.

KEEPING THEM

The Eternal One is mine. He's all I need.
I have promised to keep Your words.
PSALM 119:57 VOICE

When God sets boundaries for your time in the digital world, keep them. He knows what you need to keep a healthy perspective on social media. He knows how much television is enough, so your time together isn't breached. And the Lord knows how these can affect your heart, which is why the Holy Spirit nudges you to make changes.

Listen to those promptings. It may be a gut feeling or a warning in your heart. It may be a push to take a break. But God will make known when you're in dangerous waters because He loves you. He's your protector and strong tower. And when He speaks, follow His leading.

Dear Lord, I'm listening for Your words and will obey Your guidance. In Jesus' name, amen.

WHO ANIMATES YOUR LIFE?

If you live your life animated by the flesh—namely, your fallen, corrupt nature—then your mind is focused on the matters of the flesh. But if you live your life animated by the Spirit—namely, God's indwelling presence—then your focus is on the work of the Spirit.

ROMANS 8:5 VOICE

There's a clear distinction between living each day for the Lord or filling each day with your fleshly desires. Where our heart is, our feet will follow.

Rather than focus on the digital distractions that tempt us daily, why not put them aside and open the Bible or spend time in prayer? Why not meet a friend for coffee and talk about where God is showing up in your lives? Let the Spirit animate your life so you're focusing on the right things.

Dear Lord, let the Spirit lead me!
In Jesus' name, amen.

Rather than focus
on the digital
distractions that
tempt us daily,
why not put them
aside and open the
Bible or spend
time in prayer?

HOLY RESTRAINT

Finally, all of you, be like-minded and show sympathy, love, compassion, and humility to and for each other—not paying back evil with evil or insult with insult, but repaying the bad with a blessing. It was this you were called to do, so that you might inherit a blessing.

1 PETER 3:8–9 VOICE

Social media can be a playground for evil and insults. Chances are you've seen this before. There's a harsh boldness we sometimes feel as we sit behind a screen, typing away. And when it begins to rise up, it's time to step away.

If we're going to interact with others online, then let's show holy restraint. Let's only speak with kindness and humility. Let's respond with love and compassion. Our holy restraint will please God and bring about His blessings.

Dear Lord, help me choose to be kind online. In Jesus' name, amen.

INCORPORATING GOD

As I journey through this life, Your statutes are my song.
O Eternal One, through the night, I stop to recall Your name. That's how I live according to Your teachings.
PSALM 119:54–55 VOICE

The writer of Psalm 119:54–55 shows us how to seamlessly incorporate God into life. He went about his days, often thinking about God, His expectations, and the ways the Lord blessed his life. What if we did this too?

As we focus on projects at work, manage the family calendar, spend time with friends, and navigate the online world, let God be intertwined. Talk to Him about challenges and celebrations. Ask for guidance and wisdom. And let nothing of this world, especially digital interactions, remove the Lord from your thoughts.

Dear Lord, I want You to be part of everything I do. You're always invited into my day. In Jesus' name, amen.

EXPECTANT FOR GOD'S HAND

Just as the eyes of servants closely watch the hand of their masters, just as a maid carefully observes the slightest gesture of her mistress, in the same way we look to You, Eternal One, waiting for our God to pour out His mercy upon us.

PSALM 123:2 VOICE

When our focus isn't on screens, our eyes can be trained on the Lord instead. And the more we're in the Word and talking to Him in prayer, the deeper our relationship becomes.

Let's be expectant for God's goodness to be revealed. Rather than keep a close eye on social media or wait with anticipation for the new season of our favorite show to come out, let's meditate on scripture and await His hand to move in our lives.

Dear Lord, I want my eyes on Your goodness and not on digital distractions. In Jesus' name, amen.

WHAT DO YOU DESIRE MOST?

For all my wanting, I don't have anyone but You in heaven.
There is nothing on earth that I desire other than You.
I admit how broken I am in body and spirit, but God
is my strength, and He will be mine forever.

Psalm 73:25–26 voice

Is there anything on earth that you desire more than God? As believers, we want to declare a resounding, "No way!" But the truth is that few of us could actually say that.

We jump to check notifications on our phones. We want positive comments on our latest posts. We're excited for that new show on Netflix, and we spend our free time giggling at videos on TikTok. If this describes you, consider taking a break from screens until the Savior is your top priority once again.

Dear Lord, help me desire You most.
In Jesus' name, amen.

ROTTEN WORDS

Don't let even one rotten word seep out of your mouths. Instead, offer only fresh words that build others up when they need it most. That way your good words will communicate grace to those who hear them.

EPHESIANS 4:29 VOICE

Does social media frustrate you more than it allows you to unwind? Are you tempted to vent or respond harshly when someone shares a differing opinion? Are you intolerant of others or do you sit in judgment? Do you gossip about what you've seen online about someone? Maybe it's time to detox.

We're not to let one rotten word escape our mouths or our fingertips. As believers, we should be aware that how we treat others matters. If social media triggers you in such ways, take a break and let God tender your heart once again.

Dear Lord, help my words always be fresh and kind. In Jesus' name, amen.

THE ROAD MAP

But he's already made it plain how to live, what to do, what God is looking for in men and women. It's quite simple: Do what is fair and just to your neighbor, be compassionate and loyal in your love, and don't take yourself too seriously—take God seriously.

Micah 6:8 msg

Micah 6:8 offers a great road map for our digital interactions. By following it, we will set ourselves up for a peaceful experience without drama and angst. It may still come, but not at our hands. And if and when it does, we can remember how to respond based on this scripture.

In our interactions, let's be fair and respectful, choosing not to say hurtful or critical things. Let's use social media platforms to encourage and show kindness. And let's keep things light.

Dear Lord, help me show love, just as You command. In Jesus' name, amen.

WHAT HE REQUIRES

I will find my joy in Your commands, which I love,
and I will raise my hands to Your commands,
which I love, and I will fix my mind on what You require.
PSALM 119:47–48 VOICE

We know the Bible is full of God's commands for His children. From cover to cover, He's clear about how we're to live and what we're to avoid. But don't forget to ask the Lord to use His Spirit to guide your online life.

Are there specific social media platforms to avoid? Are there shows or channels you're not to watch? Are there times or days to power off all screens? Are there limits on how much time to spend scrolling? Or is God asking for a full detox? Today, ask Him what He requires.

Dear Lord, how do You want me to navigate
my online life? In Jesus' name, amen.

DIGITAL INTERRUPTIONS

So get yourselves ready, prepare your minds to act, control yourselves, and look forward in hope as you focus on the grace that comes when Jesus the Anointed returns and is completely revealed to you.

1 Peter 1:13 VOICE

Today's verse is a call to keep our hearts focused on God now as we look forward to the return of Jesus. It's choosing to spend our days getting ready for the Savior to come back. So whatever distractions come our way and tempt us to refocus on them instead, we're to dismiss them.

Remember, this includes digital interruptions too, especially the endless notifications we receive for text messages, social media comments, and emails. Don't let your phone interrupt your daily walk with God. Consider putting it away unless it's needed at that moment.

Dear Lord, help me put digital distractions in their place. In Jesus' name, amen.

THE RIGHT SPIRIT

You see, God did not give us a cowardly spirit but a powerful, loving, and disciplined spirit.
2 TIMOTHY 1:7 VOICE

So, because we've been given this kind of spirit, we can navigate the digital world without it ruling us. We can be wise in how much time we devote to screens and find the strength to refuse to engage in the wrong ways. We can choose to love others by how we interact online, making sure we don't have false confidence to be overtly rude or harsh (even if we feel they deserve it). And we can have the discipline to act in these ways while online.

Remember that you can choose to detox from participating in the negative side of the digital world by walking in the right spirit.

Dear Lord, help me always act in the right spirit. In Jesus' name, amen.

THE GOD OF RESTORATION

Look and see—I long for Your guidance;
restore me in Your righteousness.
PSALM 119:40 VOICE

Let's never forget that God is a God of restoration. He helps put us back on the path of righteousness when we take a wrong turn. He guides us into the right ways of living that glorify Him. The Lord directs us to walk out the calling placed on our lives. And He comforts our weary hearts as we journey together. As believers, we always have Him with us.

So, friend, let God be the one you run to when overwhelmed and overloaded by digital distractions. When you're battling the angst, cry out. He knows the posts, comments, and shows that stirred you up. He recognizes how and why they stole peace from your heart. And the Lord fully understands exactly what you need.

Dear Lord, restore me. In Jesus' name, amen.

When jealousy creeps in over what you've seen on social media, put down your phone and begin to thank God for what He's given you.

PRAY AND GIVE THANKS

Celebrate always, pray constantly, and give thanks to God no matter what circumstances you find yourself in. (This is God's will for all of you in Jesus the Anointed.) Don't suppress the Spirit.

1 THESSALONIANS 5:16–19 VOICE

When jealousy creeps in over what you've seen on social media, put down your phone and begin to thank God for what He's given you. Tell Him how grateful you are for your family and friends. Reminisce about the times He saved you, restored you, comforted you, provided for you, and blessed you unexpectedly. Show gratitude for Jesus and the Holy Spirit and how they work in your life.

One of the best ways to keep your heart focused on God's goodness is to pray and give thanks in all circumstances.

Dear Lord, Your goodness beats anything this world can offer me. In Jesus' name, amen.

ABOUT THE AUTHOR

Carey Scott is an author, speaker, and certified Biblical Life Coach who's honest about her walk with the Lord—stumbles, fumbles, and all. With authenticity and humor, she challenges women to be real, not perfect, and reminds them to trust God as their source above all else. Carey lives in Colorado with her husband. You can find her at CareyScott.org.